SPICE KITCHEN

HEALTHY LATIN AND CARIBBEAN CUISINE

CHEF ARIEL FOX

FOREWORD BY GORDON RAMSAY

For Mimi, the OG chef in my family; to my mom, the next-generation Mimi; and to my little Charlotte Grace. May you one day make me a Mimi too.

TABLE OF CONTENTS

FOREWORD

Ariel Fox is a force to be reckoned with in the kitchen. I knew from the first time she stepped into *Hell's Kitchen* in 2009 that she had talent, drive, and passion. Her tremendous talent propelled her to the top three on Season 6, and then to taking the crown on Season 18.

From that first challenge to her last, I knew that she had incredible passion for her roots in Latin and Caribbean cooking. To see her finally put that passion into a book like this is extraordinary.

Spice Kitchen will transport you to the Caribbean, a place I know well from my time working as a young chef below deck. The ingredients, the seafood, and the flavors of Caribbean food were amazing, and with her fantastic recipes Ariel will take you to the place and food I fell in love with. Ariel's passion for flavor comes through in every creation. And just because the word *healthy* is in the title doesn't mean she's cut flavor. I can guarantee you there is flavor in every bite. As someone who's competed in many Ironman competitions, I know firsthand the importance of eating and cooking healthy. The one thing I've never sacrificed is flavor, and neither does Ariel.

I would trust Ariel to run any of my kitchens around the world, so of course I trust her to make the most incredible and delicious recipes for you to cook in her cookbook. I know I'll be cooking Tana and Oscar many of these delicious treats.

Enjoy!

Gordon

THE RIGHT STUFF

To make great healthier Latin and Caribbean food, these are some of my go-to ingredients that I keep around most of the time. I try to buy the cleanest foods possible, and when in doubt, fresh is usually the best. I stay away from poorly processed foods, and most of these ingredients can be found in the grocery store. Some items are easier to find online or in your local ethnic markets. And these days, nothing is more than a click away from being delivered right to your doorstep!

Great cooking (to put it simply) is harnessing the ability to maximize flavor with balance, delivering compatible flavors that awaken the taste buds. What I love most about the cuisines of my heritage is that the combinations of ingredients almost always find a way of harmonizing the four basic tastes, and then some. Not only do we deliver sweetness, saltiness, sourness, and bitterness, but we also explore mouthfeel through texture and contrasting temperatures, aroma, and umami. Above all, the introduction to piquancy is what really sets this world of food apart.

In this section, the pantry and countertop areas refer to nonrefrigerated ingredients and make up the bulk of what we will use in this book. By no means must you keep on hand every type of alternative flour, salt, sweetener, etc. The recipes have been written using the versions that work best, but most can be swapped. At the very least, I suggest one of the staple subs.

The authenticity of the flavors in this book are rooted in traditions that may be new to you. However, through the ingredients, techniques, and recipes to follow, I hope you find new opportunities to experiment with these healthier variations—making Latin and Caribbean cuisine finally become a staple of your kitchen.

GO-TO INGREDIENTS

In the Pantry:

The Flours:
There are a ton of alternative flours on the market these days, with lots of low-calorie and gluten-free options. All will react a little differently, depending on their application, so each recipe will let you know which is best. Bob's Red Mill has a great variety of all flours.

Here is the breakdown:

Almond – Most nut flours are interchangeable and made from grinding leftover nuts. High in protein, gluten-free, low carb, higher in calories.

Banana – Made from milled dehydrated green bananas. Low calorie, gluten-free, great for baking.

Coconut – Made from dried coconut meat. High in protein, fiber, and good fat; gluten-free, great for pancakes.

Cassava – Made by grating and drying cassava root. Most interchangeable with wheat flour; not low carb, though, so should be cut with nut or coconut flour. Gluten-free, high in fiber, high in iron.

Arrow Root Starch – Alternative to cornstarch, used as a thickener. Gluten-free, paleo, great for making things crispy and crunchy, frying alternative to flour in batters.

Nuts and Seeds:
When enjoyed in moderation, nuts provide great flavor and texture, and are packed full of various heart-healthy nutrients, vitamins, and minerals, as well as omega-3 fatty acids, proteins, and more. Nuts and seeds are super versatile and are used a lot in this book: raw, in baking, in salads, in granola, and as a garnish.

A few quick notes:

Raw Almonds, Whole and Sliced – Related to the stone fruit, one of the lowest calorie nuts, high in fiber, rich in antioxidants, great for keto cooking.

Raw Cashews – High in good fats; high in magnesium and iron; great for eye, heart, and blood health; slightly sweet and buttery flavor.

Pine Nuts – Actually a seed, high in potassium, appetite suppressing, savory buttery flavor.

Sunflower Seeds – High in vitamin E and B vitamins; help prevent cardiovascular diseases and lower cholesterol; great for adding to cereals and snack mixes.

Pepitas (Pumpkin Seeds) – High in antioxidants; good source of phosphorus and magnesium; excellent when toasted, added to baked goods, or eaten as a snack.

Chia Seeds – Considered a superfood; rich in fiber and good fats; can be used as an egg alternative when ground with water; great when added to smoothies or sprinkled on baked goods.

Gluten-Free Oats – Oats that have not been contaminated with gluten in the rolling process; appetite-suppressing, lowers blood pressure, helps reduce risk of type 2 diabetes (I use quick cooking).

Blonde Quinoa – Part of the amaranth family, several B vitamins, gluten-free, high in protein.

Norwegian Crisp Breads – Low-carb and gluten-free toast and cracker alternative, made with nuts and seeds (I use Trader Joe's brand).

Sweeteners:
It can be tough to avoid sugar altogether. By avoiding processed foods and sweetened drinks, you have already won half the battle. Fortunately, there is a wide array of sugar substitutes and sweeteners, a lot of which are natural, but I have also included a few artificial as well. Not only is it important to reduce sugar intake for weight maintenance, it is also a huge factor in preventing diabetes and heart disease. Sugar can also have a negative effect on cognitive processes, affecting memory function. It can be difficult to navigate through all the alternatives, but the recipes will clearly recommend what to use and when. I keep a few on hand, most can easily be purchased online from sources such as Thrive Market.

Coconut Sugar – Natural, unrefined so it retains all of its vitamins and minerals, can be used as a straight replacement to granulated sugar, should be used in moderation, not a low-calorie sweetener.

Natural Stevia – Natural plant extract, little to no calories, much sweeter than sugar so usage is less, powder and liquid forms, does have slight aftertaste.

Monk fruit Sugar – Natural extract, much sweeter than sugar so usage is a lot lower, zero calories, does have a slight aftertaste.

Monk fruit Maple – A low-calorie alternative to real maple syrup made with monk fruit sugar and maple flavor (I use Lakanto brand).

Pure Maple Syrup – Natural, rich in minerals, high water content, used in savory and sweet applications, not a low-calorie sweetener.

Agave – Natural, sweeter than honey so you can use less, long shelf life, liquid form, not a low-calorie sweetener.

Honey – Natural, high in antioxidants, easy to digest, higher water content in liquid form, sweeter than sugar, not a low-calorie sweetener.

Pomegranate Molasses – Natural, rich in B vitamins and niacin, made by reducing real pomegranate juice down to a thick syrup, lower in calories, slightly tangy. Swerve, Brown or Powdered (does contain some erythritol) – Not a natural sweetener, sugar alcohols should be consumed in moderation, mostly recommended for baking in some recipes where natural sweeteners might not work as well.

Fats:

Saturated fats are a thing of the past and are really no longer necessary in the kitchen. Almost any recipe can be substituted with a healthier fat alternative. I love butter just as much as the next chef, and occasionally I will indulge, but there are some great products out there now that work really well, even in baking! Bottom line: cooking just isn't as great without fat. When used in moderation, there is nothing unhealthy about these fats.

Coconut Oil, Virgin – Dairy-free, solid at room temperature, can be used in baking and cooking, does have a coconut aftertaste, should be used in moderation.

Avocado Oil – A heart-healthy oil, helps the body to absorb other vitamins and minerals, high smoke point, liquid form similar to olive oil.

Olive Oil – Best used for sautéing in place of butter or canola and vegetable oils, not the best substitute for baking, some cardiovascular health benefits.

Organic Coconut Shortening – Consistency of soft butter, use in place of Crisco, creates flaky pastries.

Grass-Fed Ghee – Essentially clarified butter with the milk solids removed, dairy-free, solid at room temperature so can be used in baking in place of butter, high smoke point, good for high-temperature cooking.

Avocado and Coconut Oil Sprays, 100% Pure – Use in place of canola oil sprays.

Salts:

The primary role of salt in cooking is to enhance the flavors. Layering salt throughout the cooking process will always amplify your flavors better than waiting to season your food at the end. Our bodies actually need salt frequently, as we can't really store it. I prefer to use natural salt sources over iodized table salt. Table salt also has a distinct taste that alters your food rather than the subtle enhancing qualities of natural salts. I use mostly these four:

Sea Salt, Fine – I like fleur de sel for finishing and sauces, and less expensive Baleine for bulk usage, such as seasoning blanching water.

Sea Salt, Coarse – I use Oaxacan coarse sea salt, such as Aztec.

Sea Salt, Flake – I like Maldon.

Himalayan Pink Salt – Great for layering flavor throughout cooking, too strong as a finishing salt, any pure brand will do.

Spices:
The heart of Latin and Caribbean cooking, spices can best be broken down into flavor profiles: nutty, sweet, acidic, fruity, warm and earthy, bitter, piquant, and pungent. These are the best ways to describe spices. I have noted these nuances for each of my staple spices below:

Allspice – pungent

Cumin – warm and earthy

Cloves – pungent

Coriander – warm and earthy, sweet

Cinnamon – sweet

Ginger – pungent

Mexican Oregano – technically a dried herb, citrusy

Paprika – sweet

Curry Powder – warm and earthy

Chile flakes – piquant, heat

Fresh Pepper in Grinder – pungent

Sesame – nutty

Other Pantry Staples:

Here are a few other items I keep on hand most of the time and are used throughout the rest of the book. Most can be found at Trader Joe's, online at Thrive Market, or in ethnic markets.

Canned Prepped Green Jackfruit (I use Trader Joe's brand)

Canned Coconut Cream

Canned Coconut Milk

Cacao Nibs and Chips

Dark Chocolate

Spanish Green Olives

Capers

Most often people make the mistake of putting *everything* in the fridge. There are quite a few fruits and vegetables that should actually be stored at room temperature. Not only does the harsh cold temperature of your fridge prevent these fruits and vegetables from continuing to ripen to their peak, it also slowly changes their chemistry. The water content begins to transform from within. As long as your home's temperature is regulated during the warm summer months, you won't have to worry about attracting pests. Plus, your fridge will be a lot less cluttered, and you will have a year-round display of beautiful seasonal items.

Fruits:

Papayas

Avocados

Plantains, Green and Ripe

Dragon Fruit

Pomegranates

Berries

Cantaloupe

Vegetables:

Tomatoes

Tomatillos

Pumpkins

Spaghetti Squash

Chayote; Cho Cho

Yucca Root

Onions

Garlic

Lots of Peppers: Scotch Bonnet, Habanero, Serranos, Jalapeños, Bells

Lots of Living Herbs: I like using living herbs in little pots. They last a lot longer than the old picked herbs you buy at the store. You can prune what you need and keep the rest alive for weeks.

Basil

Mint

Thyme

Oregano

Chives

Cilantro

Of course there are many ingredients that must be refrigerated. I've listed most of them here:

Fruits and Vegetables:
Some fruits and vegetables will go bad and sour very quickly if left out, so these are the few that I definitely keep in the cooler. Try to keep away from the colder parts of the fridge, and remove moisture. I like to keep them in the drawers, lined with a cloth kitchen towel.

Cucumbers

Broccoli

Cauliflower

Kale

Spinach

Callaloo

Collard Greens

Lettuces

Zucchini

Lemons

Limes

Epazote

Scallions

Butters, Cheeses, Dairy/Non Dairy:
These are the non-shelf-stable fats. Although some nut milk beverages come in cartons found on shelves, most need to be refrigerated after opening:

Grass-Fed Butter – I like the Irish brands best.

Vegan Cashew Butter – I like Miyoko's Creamy; it bakes and eats so much like real butter!

Cashew Yogurt

Cream Cheese

Milk Alternatives: Almond, Cashew, Macadamia, Coconut
I refer to these as *carton* nut milk beverages in the recipes, not to be confused with canned coconut milk.

Cotija Cheese

Queso Fresco

Proteins:

Sourcing your proteins is one of the most important aspects of a healthier lifestyle. It is tempting to purchase lower grade proteins due to the significant price difference, but the introduction of unknown hormones, additives, and nitrates can be really harmful to the body, especially in growing children. Try to use reputable clean sources. Sustainability is also important to me. Pick and choose your battles though. Do what you can, when you can, with the resources you have. Purchasing is only half the formula; how you cook is the other half.

Organic Pasture-Raised Eggs

Grass-Fed Beef Products

Organic Pasture-Raised Chicken Products: Breasts, Thighs, Ground

Smoked Nitrate-Free, Uncured, Sugar-Free Bacon

Wild Pole Caught Fish

Other:

Raw Almond Butter

Mustard, Dijon, and Whole Grain

Avocado Oil or Olive Oil Mayo

Apple Cider Vinegar

MUST HAVE KITCHEN AND PANTRY TOOLS

- Chef Knife
- Serrated Knife
- High Heat Rubber Spatula
- Wooden Spoon
- Whisk
- Tongs
- Mortar and Pestle
- Cast Iron Pan
- Non-Stick Pan
- Large Soup Pot
- Roasting Pan
- Blender
- Baking Ware: Baking Sheets, Loaf Pan, Bundt Pan, Cake Pan, Muffin Pan, Ramekins
- Stand Mixer or Handheld Electric Mixer
- Food Mill or Handheld Potato Press
- Box Grater
- Micro plane or Zester
- Peeler
- Measuring Cups and Spoons
- Parchment Paper
- Aluminum Foil

THE RECIPES

MORNINGS

Who has time for breakfast? For whatever reason, we have neglected this beloved meal, the *breaking* of our nightly *fast*. Many people eat alone in the morning, if at all, and others are busy trying to get children up and ready for school. For a lot of families, a proper breakfast is a luxury reserved for Sunday mornings, if they're lucky enough to have everyone together. The easy way out for the solo weekday warrior might be a protein bar, or for moms and dads, a quick bowl of cereal for the kids. But cooking a good breakfast will set you up well for the rest of your day.

Some of these recipes are quick and easy, while others may be better suited for that Sunday morning. And for the skeptic who needs to roll out of bed and grab something on the go, some recipes in this section can be made in advance. Most importantly, I have swapped out the heavy carb-filled, sugar-loaded ingredients so popular in breakfast choices for wholesome natural foods that you can feel good about putting in your body. Of all the chapters of this book, these hacks are the most important. You will never feel like you "wasted" your calories, carbs, or fat on a morning meal that wasn't even enjoyed and didn't benefit your body or mind. After any of these morning meals, you will be able to enjoy eating the rest of your day too. These are my favorite healthy takes on some classic morning meals I enjoyed growing up.

- Granola
- Overnight Coconut and Chocolate Chia Seed Pudding
- Cassava "Sourdough" Pancakes
- Raspberry–Key Lime Morning Bread
- Warm Plantain Porridge Bowl
- Tropical Fruit Plate
- Huevos Rancheros (Santa Cruz Style)
- Cooking Eggs
    - Scrambled
    - Sunny Side Up
    - Over Easy, Medium, and Hard
    - Poached
    - Hard Boiled
- Pumpkin Pancakes
- Chocolate–Almond Butter Shake
- Tropical Papaya Smoothie
- Breakfast Salsa (Ranchero Salsa)
- Cashew (or Macadamia Nut) Cream Cheese
- Griddle Cake Casserole
- Smoked Salmon Everything Toasts
- Cayeye
- Arepas with Jackfruit "Carnitas"
- Pickled Onions and Peppers
- Avocado Toast
- Coco Cake Doughnuts
- Cashew Crema
- Dragon Fruit Preserves
- Homemade Nut Butters
    - Island Spice Cashew Butter
    - Coco-Almond Butter
    - Vanilla Ginger Macadamia Nut Butter
- Tropical Fruit Molasses
    - Dragon Fruit or Papaya Fruit Molasses
    - Pomegranate Fruit Molasses

GRANOLA

Just about everyone enjoys granola, and on those days when you don't have any spare time, it hits the spot. Having homemade granola on hand is a lifesaver. Not only is this version gluten-free, it has a fraction of the sugar found in store-bought granola, most of which contain dried fruit, which can shoot sugar content through the roof. Even fruit-free granolas often contain added sugar. This recipe mimics the tartness of added dried fruit by substituting homemade fruit molasses. The result is a crunchy, tangy, gluten-free, low-carb delight that can be enjoyed by itself, on top of yogurt, or even as a dessert with some coconut sorbet.

Preheat Oven 300°F

Yields 8 cups

- Avocado oil spray
- 4 cups gluten-free oats
- ⅔ cup sliced almonds
- ⅔ cup shelled sunflower seeds
- ⅔ cup shelled pumpkin seeds
- ⅓ cup flax seeds
- 1 cup unsweetened flaked coconut
- 1 cup freshly squeezed pink grapefruit juice or orange juice
- 1 tablespoon grapefruit or orange zest.
- ½ cup homemade Papaya Molasses or Pomegranate Molasses (p. 52)
- ½ cup melted coconut oil, melted
- 5 drops all natural liquid stevia
- 2 teaspoons ground cinnamon
- ¼ teaspoon ground allspice
- ¼ teaspoon ground nutmeg
- 1 tablespoon apple cider vinegar

Preheat the oven to 300°F. Spray two baking sheets with avocado oil spray, and line with parchment paper. Spray the top side of the paper again.

Combine the oats, almonds, sunflower seeds, pumpkin seeds, flax seeds, and coconut in a large bowl and mix well.

In a small saucepan, add the citrus juice, fruit molasses, melted coconut oil, liquid stevia, spices, and apple cider vinegar. Bring just to a boil, and remove from heat. Allow to cool slightly.

Carefully pour the hot liquid mixture into the dry ingredients and stir well to combine. Make sure the dry ingredients are well coated. Divide and spread the mixture evenly onto the greased lined baking sheets.

Bake, removing to stir every 10 minutes or so, for about 45 minutes, until beginning to brown and crisp.

Remove the granola from oven and allow to cool completely, breaking up the chunks as it cools.

Store in an airtight container at room temperature for up to 7 days, or freeze for up to 30 days.

Breakfast Tip: Top this granola with fresh dragon fruit or papaya— these tropical fruits are lower in sugar than strawberries or blueberries—and enjoy with unsweetened coconut milk or almond milk.

OVERNIGHT COCONUT AND CHOCOLATE CHIA SEED PUDDING

Timeless and versatile, these little pots of joy hit all the marks. Not only do chia seeds deliver an epic amount of nutrients for their calorie content, they are also packed with antioxidants and omega-3 fatty acids. Most of the carbs are fiber based, making it perfect for those on a keto diet. These little puddings pack a punch in flavor, too, and can be made ahead for the week. If you are not a chocolate lover, you can substitute matcha powder for the cacao/coco powder. My favorite toppers are toasted coconut, sliced bananas, pomegranate seeds, and cacao nibs.

Serves 4

- ¼ cup cacao powder or organic cocoa powder
- 4 tablespoons monk fruit maple syrup (I use Lakanto)
- ½ teaspoon ground cinnamon
- ¼ teaspoon fine sea salt
- ½ teaspoon vanilla extract
- 1 ½ cups carton coconut milk beverage, almond, or macadamia nut milk
- ½ cup chia seeds

In a blender, combine the cacao/coco powder, monk fruit maple syrup, cinnamon, sea salt, vanilla extract, and coconut milk. Blend on high about 1 minute to combine and evenly incorporate the powder into the liquid.

Pour the liquid into a bowl and stir in the chia seeds. Cover tightly with plastic wrap and refrigerate for at least 3 hours or overnight.

Divide the pudding among individual containers until ready to eat.

Breakfast Tip: Top with some of your homemade Granola (see p. 19)!

CASSAVA "SOURDOUGH" PANCAKES

One of my favorite memories of growing up in Santa Cruz, California, is driving with my parents up the coast on Sundays to eat sourdough pancakes. It took me a long time to develop a lower-carb recipe that would satisfy the mouthfeel and flavor of a grain-based sourdough pancake. This option uses flour made from cassava, a starchy fruit native to the Caribbean islands. The result is an addictive, fluffy, grain-free substitute for regular pancakes. Try topping these with homemade Dragon Fruit Preserves (p. 52) and a dollop of Plain Cashew Crema (p. 37).

Serves 2 to 4

- 1 ½ cup carton coconut milk beverage
- Juice of half a lemon
- 1 teaspoon apple cider vinegar
- ½ cup cultured dairy-free yogurt (such as coconut yogurt or cashew yogurt) or regular yogurt
- 1 cup cassava flour
- 1 cup coconut flour
- 1 teaspoon gluten-free baking powder
- ¼ teaspoon fine sea salt or pink Himalayan salt
- 2 large organic eggs
- 1 ½ teaspoons melted coconut oil or grass-fed ghee, plus more for cooking
- 1 teaspoon honey
- ¼ teaspoon vanilla extract
- Pinch of grated allspice
- Pinch of grated nutmeg

In a glass bowl or any nonreactive mixing bowl, combine the coconut milk with the lemon juice, apple cider vinegar, and cultured yogurt. Allow to sit for at least 60 minutes. If you can do this the night before, even better. It will make for a much faster morning preparation.

Combine the flours, baking powder, and salt in a separate mixing bowl and set aside.

Add the eggs, coconut oil, honey, vanilla, allspice, and nutmeg to the soured coconut milk and whisk together.

Gently fold the wet ingredients into the flour mixture until just combined. This batter will not look like a typical wet pancake batter. In fact, it will appear almost more like a soft dough. Don't worry though, when tipping the batter into the pan, it will soften and spread out.

Heat a cast iron skillet or griddle over medium-high heat (to 350°F). Add a little coconut oil to the skillet. For each pancake, spoon batter by the ¼ cupful onto the hot skillet, spreading just slightly with the back of the spoon. I recommend only cooking two or three at a time. Cook until the pancakes turn golden brown on the underside and batter begins to bubble in the center, about 2 minutes. Flip over, and cook for 2 minutes more. It's important never to flip pancakes after the first time; this will flatten them out. Repeat with the remaining pancake batter.

RASPBERRY-KEY LIME MORNING BREAD

This recipe is an ode to the oh-so-coveted raspberry muffin. Coconut morning bread and sweet breads are common staples in both Latin and Caribbean cuisines, and I just couldn't help myself from adding the raspberries. Ever since switching to a lower-carb diet, I have missed muffins in the morning. These simple gluten-free morning loaves can be made in advance and kept wrapped, ready to be sliced and warmed for those mornings on the go. The raspberries can be swapped for blueberries or blackberries.

Preheat Oven 350°F

Makes 1 (9-inch loaf)

- Avocado oil spray
- 1 ½ sticks European-style vegan butter (I like Mykonos brand) or grass-fed dairy butter, at room temperature
- ¾ cup monk fruit sugar or 1 cup coconut sugar
- 1 teaspoon key lime zest
- 3 large organic eggs
- 1 tablespoon key lime juice
- 1 teaspoon vanilla extract
- ½ cup coconut cream
- ¾ cup coconut flour
- 1 cup almond flour
- 1 ¼ teaspoons baking powder
- ¼ teaspoon fine sea salt
- 2 large organic egg whites, beaten
- 1 ½ cups raspberries, divided

Preheat the oven to 350°F. Spray an 8 or 9-inch loaf pan with avocado oil spray. Cut a sheet of parchment about 20 inches wider than the loaf pan. Press the paper into the loaf pan, pressing firmly to smooth and secure it, allowing the excess parchment to drape over both sides. Spray the paper with avocado oil.

In a stand mixer fitted with the paddle attachment, add the softened butter, sugar, and lime zest. Beat the mixture on medium-high speed until pale and fluffy, and sugar has dissolved, about 4 to 5 minutes.

Reduce speed slightly and add the whole eggs one at a time, scraping down between additions. Continue beating until eggs are fully incorporated.

Add the lime juice, vanilla extract, and coconut cream.

In a separate bowl, stir together both flours, the baking powder, and salt. Add the dry ingredient to the wet ingredients slowly in three additions, scraping in between. Mixer can be turned off while preparing to add the dry ingredients. When ready to add the dry ingredients, set mixer to low and add. Scrape the batter into a separate bowl and set aside.

Rinse out the stand mixer bowl and dry thoroughly. Return to the stand and replace the paddle attachment with the whip attachment. Add the 2 egg whites to the stand mixer and whip on high speed to medium peaks. (The eggs are at medium peaks when they are not foamy, hold their shape well, and when the whip is lifted, the peaks curl over on themselves slightly.)

Very gently fold the whipped egg whites into the batter in the other bowl. Do not stir too hard. Add all but 2 tablespoons of the raspberries to the batter.

Pour the batter into the prepared loaf pan and bake for 15 minutes. Sprinkle the remaining raspberries over the top of the loaf. Return to the oven and bake for another 15 minutes until golden brown. Remove the loaf from the oven and cover with foil. Bake for a final 15 minutes until a knife inserted in the center comes out clean. Breads made with flour alternatives will brown faster than traditional breads, so that final stretch of baking while covered is crucial so you don't end up with a doughy, undercooked center.

Allow the bread to cool completely at room temperature before turning out of the pan.

Dessert Tip: For a not-so-guilty midnight sweet tooth trip, heat up a couple of slices of this bread and eat with a big dollop of whipped cream.

WARM PLANTAIN PORRIDGE BOWL

Although porridge was a staple for the generations before me, both on the Caribbean side and the Irish side, I never really cared for it. It wasn't till many years later, while working at a Nordic restaurant, that I discovered a whole new world of porridge bowls. I like the combination of oats and quinoa in this recipe. A mashed plantain is the base for any proper island porridge. When you close your eyes, you would swear you are eating banana bread.

Serves 2

- 1 ripe plantain (skin should be almost black)
- 1 cup carton coconut milk beverage
- 1 Earl Grey tea bag
- Pinch of fine sea salt
- 1 tablespoon coconut sugar
- ¼ teaspoon cinnamon
- ⅛ teaspoon ground cloves
- ¼ cup blonde quinoa
- ¼ cup quick-cooking gluten-free oats
- ¼ cup water (as needed)
- ¼ teaspoon vanilla extract

In a small pot, peel the plantain and mash into a pulp. Add the coconut milk, tea bag, sea salt, coconut sugar, cinnamon, and ground cloves. Bring to a boil. Stir in the quinoa and reduce to a simmer. Remove the tea bag.

Cook the quinoa until bloomed and no longer crunchy, about 20 minutes. Add the oats and cook for another 5 minutes. The mixture should be thick but not dry. If needed, stir in some water by the tablespoon as needed until desired consistency is reached. Stir in the vanilla.

Transfer the mixture to bowls. Top with Cashew Crema (see p. 37), if desired. Top with a few sprinkles of coconut sugar, a drizzle of monk fruit maple syrup, or any one of the Homemade Nut Butters (see p. 51).

TROPICAL FRUIT PLATE

Generally, I avoid eating too much fruit. While it does provide nutritional value, most fruit just has too much sugar. Instead of using high-sugar fruits like pineapples, mangos, and kiwis, I opt for papaya, dragon fruit, and pomegranate with avocado and jicama. This simple platter is taken to another level with the addition of fresh lime juice and ancho chili powder.

Serves 4

- 1 large ripe papaya, peeled, halved, seeded, and cut into ¼-inch-thick slices
  1 ripe but firm avocado, peeled, halved, and cut into ¼-inch-thick slices
- 2 dragon fruits, peeled and cut into ¼-inch disks
- 1 medium jicama, peeled, halved, and cut into ⅛-inch-thick slices
- 4 passion fruits, halved, and cut into wedges, keeping the seedy flesh intact
- Seeds of 1 pomegranate
- 1 lime
- Pinch of ancho chili powder
- Flake sea salt

Arrange the tropical fruits on an oval platter, in the order listed above, creating a layered tessellating effect. Zest the lime and set the zest aside. Squeeze the fresh lime juice all over the fruit. Dust a pinch of ancho chili powder all over the fruit. Sprinkle the lime zest all over the platter. Finish lightly with flake salt. If you use the fruits at their peak, they should be the perfect level of sweetness, but if your fruit falls short, you can sprinkle a little bit of coconut sugar all over the platter as well.

Tip: How to pick the perfect papaya

The skin on a ripe papaya should be turning yellow and orange, and you should be able to press your thumb easily into the flesh. No worries if the papayas at the store are green; they will ripen on your counter beautifully!

HUEVOS RANCHEROS (SANTA CRUZ STYLE)

Translated literally as "ranch-style eggs," this country breakfast from Sonora, Mexico, has morphed and spread far beyond the northern border, most notably to California and Texas. Each region has contributed their own flare to the dish. My favorite version comes from my hometown of Santa Cruz. There are two nonnegotiable rules no matter what variation you decide on: 1. Ranchero sauce must be made fresh; and 2. The ingredients themselves must be fresh. Other than that, make this with any style cooked egg that you want, change up the cheeses, swap in different types of tortillas—you name it.

Preheat Oven 375°F

Serves 4

- 4 (7-inch) tortillas of choice (I use grain-free almond flour tortillas)
- Avocado oil for "frying"
- 1 cup organic canned cooked black beans, drained and rinsed
- ¼ teaspoon sea salt
- ¼ teaspoon cumin
- ¼ teaspoon garlic powder
- 4 large organic eggs, scrambled (or cooked in your preferred style—see Cooking Eggs, p. 30)
- 1 recipe Breakfast Salsa (see p. 37)
- 1 avocado, thinly sliced
- 1 recipe Charred Green Onion Cashew Crema (p. 37)
- Crumbled queso fresco (optional)
- ½ bunch fresh cilantro

Preheat the oven to 375°F.

Toss the tortillas with avocado oil until they are lightly coated, and season with salt. Lay the tortillas on a baking sheet and bake until they begin to get golden and crispy, but still slightly chewy, about 10 minutes.

In a small saucepan or skillet, gently heat the beans with a few drops of water, the sea salt, cumin, and garlic powder until warmed through.

Place one tortilla on each plate and sprinkle with the black beans. Divide the eggs among the plates and spoon over the black beans. Spoon the fresh Breakfast Salsa over the cooked eggs. Top with sliced avocado and drizzle the Charred Green Onion Cashew Crema all over. If your lifestyle permits, crumble some queso fresco over the top to finish and garnish with fresh sprigs of cilantro.

COOKING EGGS

On most mornings, a simple, perfectly prepared egg is enough to start the day. Once you learn how to cook eggs properly, you will truly become a better cook overall. Learning the restraint it takes to cook eggs over gentle heat, while understanding when to lightly manipulate them from start to finish, is no small feat! So here are a few basics before you start. You will need a good nonstick pan, one that has been cared for and washed by hand and never scratched with metal utensils. I prefer nontoxic pans with natural Thermolon coating. You will also need a high heat–tolerant rubber spatula, a small dish to crack your eggs into before you cook them (so you can remove any shells and check for impurities), and lastly, some good sea salt and grass-fed butter (you can sub vegan cashew butter or coconut shortening if you must).

Scrambled Eggs:

Scrambled eggs have only a short window when they are just right, between runny and still raw and tight-firm and rubbery. Try to serve them immediately or at least slide them onto your plate quickly when they reach this moment; never leave them in the pan.

Serves 2

- 2 teaspoons unsalted grass-fed butter (or vegan cashew butter)
- 4 large organic eggs
- Sea salt to taste

Heat an 8-inch nonstick pan over medium heat. Add the butter, let it begin to melt, but do not brown.

Crack the eggs into a small bowl and remove any shells or impurities. Lightly beat the eggs with a fork, just enough to break up the yolks and gently combine with the egg whites.

Add the eggs to the pan just before the butter is completely melted, along with a pinch of sea salt. Using a rubber spatula, immediately stir the eggs with a touch of speed, mixing until the yolks and whites are blended.

Continue to cook, removing the pan from the heat periodically, as you gently stir the eggs in a folding motion each time they begin to set around the edges. When there is only a small amount of liquid left on the base of the pan, remove the eggs from heat, and fold them one or two times more. If you are adding cheese to your eggs, add it right before you remove the eggs from the heat for the last time, but before you give them the final folds. Perfect scrambled eggs should still be a touch glossy, not pale matte yellow.

Slide the eggs onto a plate immediately and finish with another pinch of sea salt.

Sunny Side Up:

Probably the easiest method of cooking eggs, low and slow is the name of the game here. Do not try to rush sunny-side-up eggs. Cooking them too quickly will give you fried eggs on the bottom and raw, runny egg whites in the center. It is also important that you don't season the eggs until you are ready to serve them. The salt will cure the yolks, discoloring them with speckles.

Serves 2

- 2 teaspoons coconut oil, ghee, or avocado oil
- 4 large organic eggs
- Flake salt (just before serving)

Add the oil to a cold 8-inch nonstick skillet. Place the skillet over medium-low heat.

Crack 2 of the eggs into a small bowl and remove any shells or impurities. Check to make sure the yolks didn't burst. Gently slide eggs into the skillet. If the eggs begin to spatter at all, immediately remove the skillet from the heat and allow to cool slightly.

Continue to cook the eggs slowly, reducing the heat to low, until the whites are set from the edge of the yolks out, about 4 minutes. Continue to pull the pan off heat when needed if any bubbling occurs.

Once the whites are set and the yolks are glossy and still bright yellow, shake the skillet a few times to make sure the eggs are not stuck to the bottom. There should be no browning at all.

Slide the eggs onto a plate, wipe the skillet out with a paper towel, and repeat for the second batch.

Season the eggs with flake salt just before serving.

Over Easy, Medium, and Hard:

Over easy eggs are all about finesse. One tiny quick movement is all it takes. Once you get it down, you will make perfect over easy eggs forever. I call it the dip, flip, and roll. It's all in the wrist! Over mediums and over hard are essentially the same recipe, just a little more time in the pan after the flip. I keep the cook time the same on the first side for all three to minimize coloring on the presentation side, and then allow the eggs to finish cooking to medium or hard on the flip side. Lastly, I always season right before the flip, and then finish with a little more salt on the presentation side.

Serves 2

- 2 teaspoons coconut oil, ghee, or avocado oil
- 4 large organic eggs
- Sea salt

Heat half of the ghee in an 8-inch nonstick pan over medium heat.

Crack two of the eggs into a small bowl and remove any shells or impurities. Check to make sure the yolks didn't burst. Gently slide eggs into the pan. If the eggs begin to spatter at all, immediately remove the pan from heat and allow to cool slightly.

Allow to cook over medium-low heat until the egg whites are fully set, from the yolks out to the edges. Shake the pan gently to make sure the eggs are not stuck to the pan. It is very important that the egg "disk" is loosened from the pan, otherwise you won't be able to flip it! Using a circular motion, jiggle the pan to try to get the egg yolks to form a line perpendicular to the handle, across the pan from left to right. This will help prevent the yolks from bursting when they hit the pan as you flip.

Lift the pan off the heat and dip your wrist just slightly, away from your body, not enough that the eggs slide up the side, or even worse, out of the pan. Season with a pinch of sea salt.

In one swift motion, flip your wrist downward away from you, then upward back toward your body in a rolling motion, returning to your original position. Do this with enough force that the eggs briefly leave the pan, just long enough to flip over and fall gently back into the pan on the opposite side. Cook for about 30 seconds more. Remove from heat and slide the eggs onto the plate. Alternatively, if you haven't quite mastered the flip, you can use a high heat rubber spatula. Gently slide the spatula under the egg, just past the center. Lift gently and flip.

Season the presentation side with a tiny additional pinch of salt.

For over medium, cook for an additional 1 to 2 minutes after the flip, and for over hard, cook for an additional 3 to 4 minutes. When gently poked with your finger, the yolks should feel firm.

Poached:

For most egg lovers, there is nothing better than breaking open that perfectly poached egg, letting the yolk ooze out onto whatever it's being served with, and then lapping it up with a piece of toast or pancake. Serving perfect poached eggs to a guest in your home or in your restaurant is very satisfying. Don't be tempted to stir the eggs in any particular pattern; less movement is better for nicely shaped poached eggs.

Serves 2

- 4 large organic eggs
- 1 quart water
- 2 teaspoons apple cider vinegar
- Sea salt and freshly cracked black pepper

Crack each egg into individual little bowls or ramekins. Bring 4 cups water to a boil in a 2-quart pot, and then reduce to a simmer. Add the apple cider vinegar to the pot.

Working one at a time, and waiting a full minute between adding the next, slowly lower each egg dish to the surface of the water, and tilt, letting the egg slide into the water. Wait a few seconds after you drop the egg in the water and then gently jiggle a spoon underneath the egg to make sure it isn't stuck to the bottom of the pot. Once you are sure the egg is floating, and at least a minute has passed, slide the next egg in on the opposite side of the pot. Continue with the next two eggs, making sure you remember the order in which you added them. I like to follow a North, South, East, West pattern and always work only four at a time.

Allow each egg to cook in the simmering water for about 3 minutes, and up to 4 minutes. Remove each egg with a slotted spoon. Gently nudge the yolk with your finger. It should feel soft, with some slight resistance from the just set whites around it. You will be able to tell if the whites aren't set. You can always drop the eggs back in the water a little longer if needed.

Plate the eggs and season with sea salt and freshly cracked black pepper.

Hard Boiled:

Oddly enough, slightly less fresh eggs tend to be easier to peel. I try not to make hard-boiled eggs with eggs that I've just purchased; I tend to wait a few days. When boiling eggs, you can do as little or as many as you wish, as long as you use the right size pot for the job. The pot should be as small as possible to fit the eggs in a single layer. This will ensure they come to a boil as quickly as possible. Because this recipe works on a timer, it's important to not overfill the pot with water.

Serves 6

- 6 large organic eggs
- Lukewarm water
- 1 teaspoon apple cider vinegar
- 1 teaspoon olive oil
- Have a kitchen timer ready and set to 15 minutes

Using a fine needle, poke a tiny hole at the large end of each eggshell. Place the eggs in a medium pot and fill with just enough water to cover the eggs by 1 inch. Add a splash of vinegar and a splash of olive oil to the water. This will help with peeling later.

Turn the heat to medium-high, starting a 15-minute timer right away from the moment the burner is turned on, and bring the eggs to a boil. Continue to cook until 10 minutes have passed on your kitchen timer. Remove the pan from the heat and allow the eggs to sit in the hot water for 5 more minutes, until the timer hits zero. The entire process from start to finish should be 15 minutes.

Using a slotted spoon, carefully remove the eggs from the pan and place in a colander in the sink. Under running cold water, quickly and carefully peel the eggs while they are still hot on the inside. Place in the refrigerator to finish cooling.

PUMPKIN PANCAKES

During the fall months, these are a favorite with the kids because they smell and taste like pumpkin pie. I often substitute pumpkin in recipes that call for butternut squash, like the Pumpkin Soup recipe in this book (p. 57). It bakes the same as butternut, giving a very similar flavor profile but with fewer carbs and more fiber. It's a win- win. Topping these pancakes with maple syrup is great, but try them with some coconut cream and a dust of cinnamon too!

Serves 2-4

- 1 (1 ½ pounds) pie pumpkin or 1 (15-ounce) can unsweetened pumpkin purée
- 2 teaspoons sea salt, divided
- 1 cup almond flour
- 1 cup coconut flour
- 2 teaspoons baking powder
- ¾ teaspoon ground cinnamon
- ½ teaspoon ground allspice
- 2 tablespoons coconut sugar or Swerve brown sugar
- ¼ cup almond milk (or any nut milk)
- ¼ cup coconut oil, melted, plus additional for cooking
- 2 large organic eggs

Peel and seed the pumpkin, if using fresh, and cut into small 1-inch pieces. Fill a medium saucepan with enough water to cover the pumpkin and add 1 teaspoon of the sea salt. Bring to a boil. Add the cubed pumpkin and boil until soft enough to mash, about 15 minutes. Drain the pumpkin into a colander and allow to sit for 5 minutes to drain thoroughly. Mash the pumpkin with a fork into a pulp, or use a food mill. You should yield about 2 cups purée. Set aside.

In a medium mixing bowl, combine the remaining 1 teaspoon sea salt, the flours, baking powder, cinnamon, allspice, and sugar.

In a separate bowl, whisk together the nut milk, oil, and eggs.

Slowly fold the wet nut milk mixture into the dry ingredients. The batter will be slightly lumpy at this point. Don't over mix.

Gently stir the smashed pumpkin into the batter.

Heat a cast iron pan or griddle over medium-high heat. Add a tablespoon of coconut oil. Cooking only 2 or 3 pancakes at a time, add 3 tablespoons of batter per pancake. Cook each pancake for 2 to 3 minutes until bubbles begin to form in the center and the edges look dry. Flip and cook for 2 minutes more without moving again.

Serve right away.

CHOCOLATE–ALMOND BUTTER SHAKE

When you grow up on a beach, you drink shakes and smoothies—it's a way of life. My first food service job was blending up shakes and smoothies in the early morning before culinary school. I didn't realize how much sugar there was in these blender breakfasts until I was much older. This healthier version hits the spot and works well for any low-carb and dairy-free diet.

Serves 1

- 1 cup filtered water
- ¾ cup almond milk or macadamia nut milk
- 1 scoop chocolate protein powder of choice
- 2 tablespoons natural almond butter or homemade Island spiced cashew butter (p. 51)
- 1 teaspoon cacao nibs
- ½ banana
- 1 tablespoon MCT oil
- 3 to 4 ice cubes

Combine all ingredients in a blender, and blend on high speed until smooth. Pour and drink!

TROPICAL PAPAYA SMOOTHIE

Papaya is such a great fruit to work with. Not only is it super delicious and versatile, papaya is an amazing source of vitamin C and vitamin E, it is full of antioxidants, and it has a lower net carb content than mangos and pineapples. Papaya is definitely a different sort of flavor than the mainstream mango or pineapple, but if you like it, I highly suggest giving it a try.

Serves 1

- ½ medium papaya, peeled, seeded, and cubed (about 1 cup)
- ½ cup nut milk or carton coconut milk beverage
- ½ cup cashew yogurt
- 1 tablespoon fresh lime juice
- 1 teaspoon coconut sugar
- ½ cup ice for blending

Combine all ingredients in a blender, and blend on high speed until smooth. Pour and drink!

BREAKFAST SALSA (RANCHERO SALSA)

Makes 2 cups

- 2 vine-ripened tomatoes or heirloom tomatoes
- 1 small white onion, peeled and roughly chopped
- 1 serrano chile pepper, stemmed and sliced (with seeds)
- 1 Scotch bonnet chile pepper, stemmed, halved, and seeded
- 2 cloves garlic, peeled
- 1 teaspoon sea salt
- ¼ teaspoon ground cumin
- ¼ bunch fresh cilantro, chopped

In a small saucepan over medium-high heat, bring 1 quart of water to a boil.

Add the whole tomatoes, onion, chiles, and garlic. Return to a boil and reduce to a simmer. Cook until the tomatoes are soft, about 5 to 7 minutes.

Drain the vegetables, reserving ½ cup of the cooking liquid, and place the drained vegetables into a blender. Add the salt, cumin, and cilantro, and blend until smooth. If you prefer the salsa to be runnier, you can add some of the cooking liquid until you reach your desired consistency.

Cool at room temperature and serve. This salsa can be refrigerated and saved for up to 2 days, but I highly recommend serving it freshly made.

CASHEW (OR MACADAMIA NUT) CREAM CHEESE

This cream cheese alternative can be used as a substitute with bagels, in the preparation of cream cheese frostings, or any other recipe that calls for cream cheese. Although this recipe is not prep intensive, it does need a lot of hang time, so plan on starting it a couple of days ahead, or just replenish and keep some on hand.

Makes 2 cups

- 2 cups raw cashews or macadamia nuts soaked in water and covered overnight in refrigerator
- 2 tablespoons plain cultured coconut-milk yogurt
- ½ teaspoon sea salt

Drain the soaked nuts and place in a high-powered blender. Blend on high speed, scraping down occasionally, until smooth. Add a tablespoon of cold water as needed to help blend, but be careful not to add too much, or your cream cheese will be runny.

Add the yogurt and sea salt, and pulse until just combined. Transfer the mixture to an airtight container and refrigerate overnight. Allowing the cream cheese to sour and set for a full 24 hours will yield the best results.

Once the base is made, try playing around with different flavors by folding in chopped charred green onions or roasted garlic.

GRIDDLE CAKE CASSEROLE

There was a time when I was slinging griddle cakes in a pop-up stand in Williamsburg every weekend to make ends meet. Anyone who knows me well knows about my original griddle cakes. I've had to reinvent the recipe over the years to work with my healthier lifestyle shift, substituting Kiss My Keto bread for the original challah and sourdough. Although this isn't the OG griddle cake recipe, this delicious version satisfies all the same cravings without the guilt. If you can prepare this up to the point of cooking the night before, it will come out even better.

Preheat Oven 350°F

Serves 2-4

- Avocado or coconut oil spray
- ¾ cup finely ground almond flour
- 2 tablespoons coconut sugar or monk fruit sugar substitute
- 1 tablespoon gluten-free baking powder
- ½ teaspoon fine sea salt
- 8 ounces Kiss My Keto bread
- 2 cups carton coconut milk beverage
- ½ teaspoon vanilla extract
- Zest of 1 orange
- 4 large organic eggs, beaten
- 5 tablespoons coconut oil, melted, or grass-fed ghee

Spray a 9 × 13-inch baking dish or a 9-inch cast iron skillet with avocado oil or coconut oil spray.

In a medium mixing bowl, combine the almond flour, sugar, baking powder, and sea salt. Set aside.

In a separate large bowl, tear the bread into rough 1-inch pieces. Set aside.

In a third small bowl, whisk together the coconut milk, vanilla, orange zest, and eggs until well combined.

Gently fold about half the dry ingredients into the torn bread, followed by half of the wet ingredients. Repeat with the second half of the dry ingredients followed by the remaining wet ingredients. Stir in the coconut oil.

Pour the mixture into the greased dish, cover with foil, and refrigerate for a minimum of 30 minutes, or prep up to this point and refrigerate overnight.

Preheat the oven to 350°F.

Bake the foil-covered casserole for 30 minutes. Remove the foil and continue to cook until fluffy and lightly browned, about 15 minutes more.

Serve in the dish or skillet dusted lightly with powdered stevia sugar and monk fruit maple syrup.

SMOKED SALMON EVERYTHING TOASTS

There are few morning flavor combinations I adore more than a smoked salmon everything bagel with all the fixings: capers, thinly sliced red onion, and tomatoes. I gave up my bagel obsession for a healthier lifestyle, but I still enjoy this heavenly flavor combo. These little Norwegian crisp breads are a great substitute for toasts and crackers. The homemade Cashew Cream Cheese is a wonderful substitute for the dairy variety too.

Serves 1

- 4 tablespoons homemade Cashew Cream Cheese (p. 37) or dairy cream cheese
- 2 gluten-free Norwegian crispbreads
- 2 large organic eggs, hard-boiled, peeled, and sliced (see Cooking Eggs, p. 34)
- Sea salt and freshly cracked black pep per to taste
- 4 slices smoked salmon
- ¼ of a small red onion, very thinly sliced
- ½ of a vine-ripe or heirloom tomato, very thinly sliced
- 1 teaspoon capers
- 1 teaspoon fresh dill fronds
- 1 teaspoon extra-virgin olive oil
- ½ teaspoon "everything" spice mix (I use Thrive Market)

To assemble the toasts, evenly divide and spread the cashew cream cheese over each crispbread.

Arrange the hard-boiled egg slices on top of the cream cheese and season with a pinch of sea salt and freshly cracked pepper.

Next, layer the toasts with ribbons of smoked salmon slices.

Top with sliced onion, tomato crescents, capers, and dill.

Drizzle with extra-virgin olive oil, and sprinkle all over with everything spice mix and enjoy!

CAYEYE

This dish is known by many names throughout Latin cultures and the Caribbean islands. In Cuba they call it *fufu*; in the Dominican Republic, *mangu*; and in Puerto Rico, where it is the national dish, *mofongo*. Cayeye is the Colombian name. It is most commonly eaten for breakfast and topped with eggs. What I love about this dish is that you can also make it with yucca root or cho cho (chayote) for a lighter take.

Serves 4

- 4 green plantains or yucca roots
- Water to cover
- 1 ¾ teaspoons sea salt, divided
- 3 tablespoons coconut oil
- 1 medium yellow onion, diced fine into ¼-inch pieces
- 4 green onions, sliced, green and white parts
- 1 Scotch bonnet chile pepper, stemmed, seeded, and diced fine into ¼-inch pieces
- 2 cloves garlic, minced
- ½ teaspoon achiote paste
- ¼ teaspoon ground cumin
- 2 vine-ripened or heirloom tomatoes, diced into ½-inch pieces
- ⅛ cup coconut oil, grass-fed ghee, or vegan cashew butter
- ¼ cup cold water
- 4 eggs, cooked any style
- 1 avocado, sliced thin
- 4 tablespoons Cashew Crema (p. 37)
- 4 tablespoons queso fresco, crumbled

Prepare the Plantains: Peel the plantains by first cutting off the ends and then cutting a slit lengthwise down the plantain. Peel back the skin from the flesh of the plantains. Cut the peeled plantains in half lengthwise, then into 1-inch pieces, and place in a wide, medium-size pot. Fill the pot with just enough water to cover the plantains, about 1 to 2 inches up the side. Season with ¼ teaspoon of the sea salt. Turn the heat on high and bring to a boil. Boil the plantains for about 20 minutes, until fork tender. The same cooking method can be used if using yucca instead of plantains, first peeling off the rough brown skin. Boil the yucca for about 30 minutes, until fork tender.

Meanwhile, in a medium (preferably nonstick) skillet, heat the 3 tablespoons of coconut oil over medium heat. Add the yellow onion, green onions, Scotch bonnet chile pepper, and about ½ teaspoon of sea salt and sauté until the onion is translucent and tender, about 4 or 5 minutes. Reduce the heat to low and add the garlic. Cook for 1 minute more. Stir in the achiote paste, cumin, and tomatoes. Cook for 2 minutes more. Turn off the heat but keep warm until the plantains are ready.

Once the plantains are tender, drain them and place them in a bowl. Add ⅛ cup coconut oil or good fat of your choosing, and the remaining 1 teaspoon sea salt. Mash with a fork or starch masher. Once the fat has fully been incorporated into the plantains, add the cold water and continue to mash until the plantains are creamy. If needed you may add additional cold water until the desired consistency is reached.

Finally, fold the warm onion-tomato mixture into the plantain mixture.

Divide and serve topped with preferred style of eggs (see egg cooking), sliced avocado, Cashew Crema (p. 37), and if your nutritional lifestyle permits, some crumbled queso.

AREPAS WITH JACKFRUIT "CARNITAS"

Arepas are a staple in Colombian cuisine, and for breakfast, they are typically piled high with braised meats, cheese, and eggs. While I do eat these with meat, in this recipe I use a delicious meat alternative called jackfruit. It is best to work with canned green jackfruit—all the work is done for you and it is safe to eat, unlike the fresh raw fruit that can be toxic at different stages of its growth. Jackfruit, known as breadfruit in the islands, makes a wonderful vegetarian filling for just about anything.

Preheat Oven 350°F

Serves 4

Arepas:

- ¾ cup coconut flour
- ¾ cup arrowroot starch
- ½ teaspoon cream of tartar
- ¼ teaspoon baking powder
- ½ teaspoon fine sea salt
- 2 tablespoons coconut shortening
- 1 large organic egg, beaten
- 1 tablespoon cold water
- 1 tablespoon coconut oil for cooking

Jackfruit "Carnitas":

- 2 (15-ounce) cans green jackfruit, drained and rinsed
- 2 tablespoons coconut oil
- 1 cup yellow onion, peeled and finely diced into ¼-inch pieces
- 4 cloves garlic, minced
- 1 serrano chile pepper, seeded and minced
- 1 tablespoon chili powder
- 1 teaspoon Goya Sazón seasoning
- 1 teaspoon ground cumin
- Pinch of cinnamon
- 1 teaspoon dried oregano
- 1 teaspoon minced epazote leaf (optional)
- ½ teaspoon sea salt
- ½ cup water
- Additional sea salt and freshly cracked black pepper to taste

Preheat the oven to 350°F.

For the Arepas: In a mixing bowl, combine the coconut flour, arrowroot starch, cream of tartar, baking powder, and salt. Using a pastry cutter or two forks, cut the coconut shortening into the dry ingredients until the texture resembles moist soil. Add the egg and 1 tablespoon cold water. Start folding until a uniform dough is formed. Allow to rest for 10 minutes. Divide the dough into 4 portions. Roll each portion into a ball and flatten it to make a ½-inch-thick disk.

Heat a large cast-iron skillet over high heat and add the coconut oil. Cook the arepas for 3 to 4 minutes per side until lightly browned. Transfer the skillet to the oven and continue to cook the arepas for about 10 minutes until golden brown and cooked through. Lower the oven temperature to 200°F, and keep the arepas warm while preparing the carnitas.

Make the "carnitas": Using your fingers, tear apart the jackfruit into a consistency like pulled pork.

Heat a medium skillet over medium-high heat. Add 2 tablespoons coconut oil. Add the onion and garlic and sauté for 2 to 3 minutes. Add the serrano chile. Add the jackfruit and remaining ingredients. Reduce heat to low and cook anywhere from 4-6 minutes, until the jackfruit easily pulls apart with a fork . Season to taste with additional salt and black pepper if desired.

Place one arepa on each plate and top with the jackfruit mixture. If you like, add eggs cooked any style and some melted cheese. I like to place a slice of Mexican queso enchilado over eggs and broil until just melted.

PICKLED ONIONS AND PEPPERS

I could put these on just about anything. Acid and heat are a fantastic complement to just about any savory Latin or Caribbean dish. I often put these out on the table as a side dish.

Makes 1 quart

- 12 medium shallots, peeled and cut into ⅛-inch slices
- 4 Scotch bonnet chile peppers, halved, seeded, and thinly sliced
- 1 teaspoon grated fresh ginger root
- 1 clove garlic, peeled and grated
- 2 bay leaves
- 1 teaspoon whole allspice berries
- 2 cups apple cider vinegar
- 1 tablespoon coconut sugar
- ½ teaspoon sea salt
- 1 teaspoon coriander seeds

Place the shallots and Scotch bonnet chile peppers in a clean sanitized jar. In a small pot over medium-high heat, combine the remaining ingredients and bring to a boil. Pour the mixture over the shallots and peppers. Allow to cool completely at room temperature before closing the jar and refrigerating. Allow to pickle for at least 4 hours before using, a full day is best. Store refrigerated for up to 1 month.

AVOCADO TOAST

You can't grow up in California without eating avocado toast. Even in the islands, the avocado fruit is part of daily eating. Every part of my heritage cherishes avocados, so it's no wonder they are a staple in my kitchen.

Serves 1

- 1 large ripe avocado, peeled and seeded
- Flake sea salt to taste (I like Maldon)
- 2 tablespoons fresh cilantro leaves
- 2 tablespoons fresh mint leaves
- 1 tablespoon chopped chives
- 1 tablespoon chopped green onions
- 1 clove garlic, peeled and grated or minced
- 1 serrano chile pepper, stemmed, seeded, and finely diced
- Squeeze of fresh lime juice
- 2 pieces gluten-free Norwegian crisp bread or keto bread (I like Kiss My Keto)
- 2 large pinches pickled onions and peppers (p. 46)
- Extra-virgin olive oil for drizzling

In a small mixing bowl, place avocado pulp. Add the sea salt to taste, herbs, scallions, garlic, serrano chile, and lime juice. Mash gently with a fork until the consistency of guacamole is reached. There should be a few chunks of avocado not broken down completely.

Divide and spread the avocado mixture over the crispbread. Top each one with a pinch of the Pickled Onions and Peppers. Drizzle with olive oil.

COCO CAKE DOUGHNUTS

I know that there is no healthy substitute for the puffy fried American-style doughnut or sopapillas found in Mexico. But cake-style doughnuts have long been enjoyed in the Caribbean, and this healthier version hits the spot. The addition of avocado adds a much-needed layer of moisture you won't find in most alternative doughnut recipes.

Preheat Oven 375°F

Makes 6 doughnuts

Doughnuts:

- Coconut oil spray or avocado oil spray
- 3 large organic eggs
- ¼ cup coconut sugar or monk fruit sugar
- ¼ cup coconut cream
- ½ ripe avocado, peeled and roughly chopped
- 1 teaspoon vanilla extract
- ½ cup finely ground almond flour
- ½ cup coconut flour
- 1 tablespoon cocoa powder
- 2 teaspoons baking powder

Frosting:

- 1 cup sugar-free chocolate chips (such as Lily's Dark Chocolate Chips)
- 2 tablespoons coconut oil

Preheat the oven to 375°F. Grease a nonstick doughnut pan with coconut oil spray.

Make the doughnuts: In a stand mixer fitted with the whip attachment, whip the eggs, sugar, coconut cream, avocado, and vanilla until fully combined and smooth, approximately 5 minutes.

In a separate medium bowl, combine the dry ingredients and gently fold into the wet ingredients using a rubber spatula until a batter is formed.

If you have a piping bag, pour the batter into a piping bag and pipe even rings of batter into the greased doughnut pan. The tubes of batter should be about 1 inch in diameter. If you don't have a piping bag, you can spoon the batter into a Ziploc bag and seal it, squeezing out as much air as possible. Cut a small hole at the corner of the bag, about 1 inch in diameter. Gently squeeze the batter as you would the piping bag.

Bake the doughnuts for about 20 minutes, or until the doughnuts become cakelike, risen and firm. Allow the doughnuts to cool in the pan for 10 minutes before popping them out. Allow them to cool completely before frosting.

Make the frosting: Place the chocolate chips and coconut oil in a metal mixing bowl. Bring a small pot of water to a boil and remove from heat. Place the bowl over the pot, off the heat. Stir until the chocolate is melted and combined with the coconut oil. Alternatively, place the chocolate chips and coconut oil in a microwave safe bowl. Heat for 30 seconds at a time, stirring in between, until the mixture is just melted and smooth. Do not overcook. One at a time, dip the doughnuts into the melted chocolate mixture. Place the dipped doughnuts on a rack to allow the frosting to set.

Cashew crema is a great alternative to a Mexican-style crema, sour cream, or French-style crème fraîche. It can be easily adjusted in texture by adding a touch of cold water and whisked in if looser consistency is called for such as drizzling over a soup.

Makes 1 cup

Plain Cashew Crema:

- 1 cup raw cashews
- ½ cup filtered water

Makes ½ cup

Charred Green Onion Cashew Crema:

- ½ cup prepared Cashew Crema
- 4 green onions, trimmed
- Juice and zest of 1 lime
- Pink Himalayan salt to taste

Makes 1 ½ cup

Avocado and Scotch Bonnet Cashew Crema:

- 1 ripe avocado, halved, and pitted
- ½ scotch bonnet pepper, stemmed and seeded
- 1 cup prepared Cashew Crema
- 2 tablespoons avocado oil
- 1 teaspoon honey
- 1 teaspoon Sea Salt

Plain Cashew Crema: Place cashews and water in a high-powered blender. Blend on high until completely smooth.

Charred Green Onion Cashew Crema: Char the green onions whole over an open flame for about 3 or 4 minutes. You can do this right over the burner on your stove. Make sure to turn them frequently. Allow to cool slightly before chopping to a fine pulp. Fold the charred onions, lime juice, and lime zest into the crema. Season with pink salt to taste.

Avocado and Scotch Bonnet Cashew Crema: Combine all the ingredients in a blender and blend on high for 20 seconds. Turn off the blender and scrape down the sides to make sure all the ingredients make their way down into the mixture. Repeat this process until the crema is smooth and uniform in texture. Season to taste.

All of these Cremas should be refrigerated until ready to use, for up to one week.

DRAGON FRUIT PRESERVES

I loved eating toast with butter and strawberry or apricot jams growing up, but they are so full of sugar. I love this jelly because it isn't overly sweet and doesn't require as much additional sweetener to make. The riper the fruit the better, as it gets naturally sweeter. Dragon fruit has a nice flavor profile between a pear and a kiwi.

Makes 1 ½ cups

- 2 medium dragon fruits (pink)
- Juice and zest of 1 lemon (about ¼ cup juice)
- 2 large organic egg yolks
- 2 tablespoons coconut shortening or dairy grass-fed butter
- ¼ cup coconut sugar

Cut open the dragon fruit lengthwise and scoop out the pulp. Place the fruit in a medium heatproof glass or stainless steel mixing bowl. Add the lemon juice and zest, egg yolks, coconut shortening, and coconut sugar. Whisk to combine.

Place the bowl over a pot of boiling water on medium-high heat to act as a double boiler. The bowl should nest into the pot without falling in and without touching the surface of the water, and the flames should not extend past the edges of the bottom of the pot. Cook the mixture while whisking with a wire whip constantly, until the mixture thickens and the jam has turned a pale bright purple, about 20 to 25 minutes.

Remove the bowl from the pot and place into another larger bowl filled halfway with ice water. Whisk the jam for about 5 minutes until room temperature. Place a piece of plastic wrap over the jam, pressing down to ensure that the plastic is touching the entire surface area. Place the jam in the refrigerator and allow to finish cooling and setting for at least 2 hours.

Transfer to an airtight food storage container or cleaned and sanitized glass jar. The jam should last up to 1 week.

HOMEMADE NUT BUTTERS

These rich and flavorful nut butters can be enjoyed in a variety of ways—spread on breads and toasts, blended into shakes, crumbled into yogurt, or dolloped on top of ice cream. One thing is for certain: Once you start making your own nut butters, you will have a hard time going back to the store-bought butters we are all used to.

Each recipe makes 2 cups, or 1 8-inch log

Island Spiced Cashew Butter:

• 2 cups roasted unsalted cashews

• 3 tablespoons coconut oil

• ½ teaspoon sea salt

• 1 teaspoon honey or agave nectar

• ¼ cup carton coconut milk beverage

• ⅛ teaspoon ground allspice

• ⅛ teaspoon ground cinnamon

• ⅛ teaspoon ground cloves

Cocoa Almond Butter:

• 2 cups whole roasted unsalted almonds

• ⅓ cup avocado oil

• ¼ cup cocoa powder

• ½ teaspoon sea salt

• 2 tablespoons honey or agave nectar

• ½ cup water

Vanilla Ginger Macadamia Nut Butter:

• 2 cups raw macadamia nuts

• ¼ cup coconut oil

• 1 teaspoon vanilla extract

• ½ teaspoon sea salt

• 2 teaspoons pure maple syrup or monk fruit maple syrup

• ¼ cup carton coconut milk beverage

• ⅛ teaspoon ground ginger

For each nut butter, combine all ingredients in a high-powered blender and blend until smooth. The nut butters will be slightly hot from the heat generated by the blades during blending. Remove to a bowl to cool completely. Transfer to a sanitized glass jar or container and refrigerate for up to 2 weeks until ready to use. Alternatively, you can create a log of butter for easy slicing by scooping the prepared butters onto a sheet of parchment paper. Start by scooping the butter all along one edge of a 12-inch square of parchment, leaving 2 inches on either edge. Lift the parchment paper up onto the butter and begin to roll it up into a log. Twist the ends of the paper, like a candy wrapper, tightening until the log is compacted and about 2 inches in diameter. These can be frozen for up to 3 months.

TROPICAL FRUIT MOLASSES

Makes 1 cup

Dragon Fruit or Papaya Molasses:

- 2 ½ pounds cubed very ripe dragon fruit (about 8 medium dragon fruit) or very ripe papaya (about 2 medium papaya), or 4 cups
- 1 quart raw coconut water
- 1 tablespoon coconut sugar to taste (if the dragon fruit is not very sweet naturally)
- 1 tablespoon freshly squeezed lemon juice

Makes 1 cup

Pomegranate Molasses:

- 4 cups 100% pomegranate juice (such as Pom, or juiced at home)
- 2 tablespoons coconut sugar
- 1 tablespoon freshly squeezed lemon juice

Dragon Fruit or Papaya Molasses: Place the fruit in a high-powered blender or food processor along with the coconut water. Pulse several times, for 2 seconds each time, to get as much liquid out of the fruit as possible without blending it completely into a purée.

Pour the contents of the blender through a fine mesh strainer over a medium sized pot. Using your hands, or the back of a ladle, gently press on the pulp in the strainer to extract as much juice as possible. You should have about 1 ½ to 2 quarts of liquid.

Place the pot on the stove over medium heat and bring to a simmer. Whisk in the coconut sugar (if needed) and lemon juice. Allow the liquid to cook over medium to medium-low heat for about 2 hours, until reduced to 2 cups. Frequently skim any foam or impurities that rise to the top while cooking. If the pan begins to scorch on the sides at any point during the second half of cooking, transfer the mixture to a clean pot to continue. Remove the mixture from the stove and cool for 1 hour at room temperature before transferring to a clean and sanitized glass jar or food storage container. If you aren't going to use within 30 days, you can freeze the molasses.

Pomegranate Molasses: Place the pomegranate juice in a medium pot along with the coconut sugar and lemon juice. Bring to a boil and cook the mixture over medium heat until the sugar has dissolved.

Reduce the heat to medium-low and cook about 1 to 1 ½ hours, until the mixture has thickened and reduced to 1 cup. Frequently skim the surface of any foam or impurities that rise to the top while cooking. The mixture will be thick and syrupy.

Remove the molasses from heat and allow to cool at room temperature for 30 minutes. Transfer to a clean and sanitized glass jar or food storage container. Refrigerate for up to 2 weeks, or freeze for up to 3 months.

SOUPS

The most memorable and satisfying soups have always been exemplary of a region's locality and seasonality. I am particularly partial to coastal chowders and stews, from the Ron Don of my Colombian grandmother Netta's heritage to the cioppinos and bouillabaisses of my Mimi. These soups hold the key to my heart. Making soup requires patience and an understanding of how to layer flavors. Although the end result may seem so simple to the naked eye, I assure you, a good-quality soup is no small feat. Always buy what is in season, and if you live on the coast, buy local seafood. If you live in the mountains, use pasture-raised poultry and foraged ingredients. Have fun when you decide to make a soup, and get creative. There are no boundaries here! These are some of my favorites.

- Pumpkin Soup
- Posole Rojo
- Creamy Callaloo and Celeriac Soup
- Encebollado
- Seafood Chowder
- Chilled Papaya and Melon Soup
- Easy Cauliflower Cream (Heavy Cream Substitute)
- Homemade Chile Oil
- Toasted Pepitas
- Avocado, Tomatillo, and Charred Green Onion Gazpacho

PUMPKIN SOUP

I used to make butternut squash soup like most folks in the fall, but once I discovered the benefits of pumpkin, I never went back. My grandmothers used to make pumpkin soups, and they always made it from scratch. I love that fact that they used pumpkins for so many things besides pumpkin pie. This healthy, hearty soup is sure to warm the soul and can be enjoyed from late September until almost Christmas. Leaving the skin on the roasted pumpkin and blending it right into the soup not only adds a depth of flavor, but it also gives a huge boost of carotenoids, which your body turns into vitamin A. The skin also contains minerals such as zinc and copper, which promote super healthy skin! Pumpkin is seriously a wonder food, which is why I sub it in for so many squash applications. Remember, when seeding a pumpkin, save the seeds to make Toasted Pepitas (p. 65)!

 Preheat Oven 375°F

Yields 4 quarts

- Avocado oil pan spray
- 2 small pie pumpkins (about 5 pounds total), stemmed, seeded, and cut into 4 wedges with the skin on
- ¼ cup coconut oil, plus 2 tablespoons
- 2 tablespoons coconut sugar
- 1 teaspoon sea salt
- ½ teaspoon freshly cracked black pepper
- 2 cloves garlic, minced
- 1 large yellow onion, peeled and diced
- ½ cup honey or brown Swerve sugar alternative
- 1 teaspoon ground cinnamon
- ¼ teaspoon ground allspice
- ⅛ teaspoon ground cloves
- ⅛ teaspoon ground nutmeg
- 3 sprigs fresh thyme
- 2 quarts light chicken broth (or vegetable broth if keeping the soup vegetarian)
- 1 cup coconut cream
- Sea salt to taste

Garnishes:
- Cashew Crema (p. 37)
- Toasted Pepitas (p. 65)
- Homemade Chile Oil (p. 65)

Preheat the oven to 375°F. Grease a baking sheet with avocado oil spray.

Toss the pumpkin wedges with ¼ cup of coconut oil, coconut sugar, sea salt, and pepper.

Roast the pumpkin on the prepared baking sheet in the oven until fork tender and caramelized. About 1 hour.

Heat the remaining 2 tablespoons of coconut oil in a large soup pot. Add the garlic, onion, honey, and spices, and sauté for 5 to 7 minutes until the onions are tender. Add the thyme, broth, coconut cream, and roasted pumpkin, skin and all. Bring to a boil and reduce to a simmer. Cook the soup for 1 hour. Remove from heat and allow to cool slightly. Remove the thyme sprigs.

Using a high-powered blender, in small batches, carefully blend the warm soup until smooth. Return the smooth blended soup to the pot. Season to taste. This soup can be made up to 3 days ahead and heated before serving. Serve with a drizzle of Cashew Crema, some Toasted Pepitas, and a few drops of Homemade Chile Oil.

POSOLE ROJO

This is hands down my favorite stew to make. Posole is the perfect casual party meal, and it makes a beautiful presentation when you set out a giant kettle of this deep-red soup surrounded by all of the fresh fixings. It is tradition to top posole with loads of shaved fresh vegetables like radishes, cabbage, onions, jalapeños, and avocado. Then tie it all together with sprigs of fresh cilantro and wedges of lime for squeezing. I also like to drizzle in some Charred Green Onion Cashew Crema (p. 37). The hominy isn't particularly good for you, but it isn't really unhealthy in small doses. I have subbed in half the amount of hominy with black-eyed peas, which are lower in carbs and add another layer of flavor. Don't cheat yourself out of all the different chiles used below. Find a Mexican market and commit—I promise you won't be disappointed.

Serves 8

Dried Chile Paste:
- 6 dried guajillo chile peppers
- 4 dried ancho chile peppers
- 2 dried pasilla negra chile peppers
- 2 dried morita chile peppers
- 4 dried chiles de árbol
- 1 jarred chipotle pepper in adobo sauce plus 2 tablespoons adobo sauce

Stew:
- 1 (2 ½ pound) rack baby back pork ribs, cut into 2 pieces
- 8 boneless skinless chicken thighs (about 2 pounds)
- 2 tablespoons sea salt
- 1 tablespoon freshly cracked black pepper
- 2 teaspoons ground cumin
- 2 tablespoons avocado oil, plus more as needed for cooking
- 2 medium Spanish onions, peeled and diced into ½-inch pieces
- 6 cloves garlic, minced or grated
- 1 bay leaf
- 1 teaspoon dried Mexican oregano
- 2 avocado leaves, available in Mexican markets
- ¼ teaspoon ground allspice
- ¼ teaspoon ground cinnamon
- 2 quarts chicken stock or bone broth
- 2 quarts water
- 3 (15-ounce) cans cooked organic hominy, drained and rinsed
- 2 (15-ounce) cans cooked black-eyed peas, drained and rinsed
- Sea salt and pepper to taste

Suggested Fixings: shredded cabbage, shaved white onions, shaved radishes, shaved jalapeño peppers, sliced avocado, fresh cilantro sprigs, Charred Green Onion Cashew Crema (p. 37), crumbled queso fresco, plenty of lime wedges

Make the Chile Paste: Break the stems off all the chiles and shake out and discard as many of the seeds as you can. Place the stemmed and seeded dried chiles in a bowl and add enough boiling water to cover. Cover the bowl with plastic and allow the chiles to soak for at least 30 minutes, until soft. Transfer the softened chiles and chipotle peppers in adobo to a blender along with 1 cup of the soaking liquid. Blend on high speed until smooth and uniform. Press the mixture through a fine-mesh strainer to remove any bitter coarse skins left behind. Be careful not to inhale directly over the chiles while blending! Set the chile paste aside.

Make the Soup: Toss the rib pieces and chicken thighs with the sea salt, cracked black pepper, cumin, and avocado oil until well coated. Heat a large, wide-bottom soup pot over medium-high heat. In batches, being careful not to overcrowd the pot, sear the ribs and chicken thighs until deep golden brown on all sides, about 3 to 5 minutes per side. Remove the browned meat to a plate while browning the next batches. Add a little more avocado oil to the pan to keep it from scorching, and turn the heat down to medium if need be.

Once all the meat has been browned, remove it from the pot. Add the onions to the same pot and sauté until tender and translucent, about 3 to 4 minutes. Add the garlic and cook for 1 minute more. Add back in the browned meats, bay leaf, Mexican oregano, avocado leaves, allspice, and cinnamon. Pour in the 2 quarts of chicken stock and top with 2 quarts of water. Bring to a boil, then reduce heat to a simmer. Stir in the chile paste. Allow to cook for 2 ½ hours until the pork is tender and falling off the bones.

Once the pork ribs are done, carefully scoop out all of the ribs and chicken thighs from the pot onto a large cutting board. Gently pull and shred the meats and return them to the pot. Discard the bones. Add the hominy and black-eyed peas to the pot. Season to taste with salt and black pepper. Allow the soup to cook on low heat for 1 hour more.

Serve in the pot and place all of the fixings on the side for everyone to build their own bowls.

CREAMY CALLALOO AND CELERIAC SOUP

Callaloo are the leafy greens of the amaranth or taro plant found in many dishes throughout the Caribbean. This version of the popular callaloo soup is simple and can be made with any leafy greens if you can't find callaloo. I promise it's worth the trip to a Jamaican or Asian market, though, to get the genuine amaranth or taro bush greens. When buying callaloo, make sure to check the stems for freshness; they should be green and firm, not shriveled up and dry. Prep the greens by washing thoroughly and trimming off the knots, buds, and tough stem ends.

Serves 4 to 6

- 2 green plantains, peeled and sliced
- 2 medium chayote squash, peeled and cubed
- 1 medium celery root, peeled
- 1 tablespoon avocado oil
- 1 tablespoon coconut oil
- 2 medium yellow onions, peeled and diced into ½ inch pieces
- 4 cloves garlic, minced
- 1 tablespoon coconut sugar
- 4 to 6 cups callaloo or spinach, trimmed and chopped (see the recipe tip)
- 1 (15-ounce) can coconut milk
- 8 ounces chicken or vegetable broth
- 1 dried avocado leaf, available in Mexican and Caribbean markets
- 1 bunch fresh cilantro, chopped
- Sea salt and freshly cracked black pepper to taste

Garnishes:

- Fresh mint sprigs
- Plain Cashew Crema (p. 37)
- Crispy onion and/or garlic (found in most ethnic markets)
- Homemade Chile Oil (p. 65)
- plantain chips or croutons (also found in most ethnic markets)

Blanch the vegetables: Heat a medium soup pot of water over medium-high heat and season generously with sea salt. Working with one vegetable at a time, blanch the plantains, chayote squash, and celery root until fork tender, about 8 to 10 minutes each. Remove from blanching water onto a baking sheet and set aside. Discard the blanching water and clean and dry the pot.

Place the medium soup pot back on the stove and heat over medium-high heat. Add the avocado and coconut oils, onions, and garlic and sauté for 2 to 3 minutes until onions are translucent and garlic is fragrant.

Add the blanched vegetables along with the coconut sugar and continue to cook until the sugar begins to caramelize and brown in the pot, about 2 to 3 minutes more.

Add the callaloo, coconut milk, broth, and avocado leaf. Bring back up to a boil and then reduce to a low simmer, cover, and cook for 20 minutes.

Stir in the chopped cilantro and cook 5 minutes more. Remove from heat and allow to cool slightly.

In small batches, in a high-powered blender, carefully purée the soup. Adjust seasoning and serve topped with garnishes.

Tip: Prepping callaloo

1) Cut off the ends of the stems, and strip the leaves from the stalks using a small paring knife.

2) Place the leaves in a large bowl filled with water and vigorously agitate to remove any dirt or insects. Allow to sit for 5 minutes so that all the debris can settle to the bottom of the bowl. Lift the leaves out of the water and chop. They are ready to cook at this point.

ENCEBOLLADO

My husband is Puerto Rican and Ecuadorian, so it is only fitting that I feature this tasty soup made with fresh tuna and yucca root, served with pickled onions and fresh tomatoes. The soup literally translates to the word "onioned." Encebollado is the national dish of Ecuador and is enjoyed on the coast any time of day and all year round.

Serves 2 to 4

- 2 tablespoons avocado oil
- 1 medium yellow onion, peeled and diced into ½-inch pieces
- 2 cloves garlic, shaved thin
- 2 vine-ripened tomatoes, diced into ½-inch pieces
- 2 teaspoons ground cumin
- 2 teaspoons ground paprika
- 2 quarts vegetable broth or fish broth
- 1 cup chopped fresh cilantro
- 1 pound yucca root, peeled and cut into 1-inch cubes
- 2 pounds fresh tuna steak, cut into 1-inch cubes
- Sea salt and freshly cracked black pepper to taste

Garnishes:

- Pickled Onions and Peppers (p. 46)
- Diced heirloom tomatoes
- Fresh lime wedges for squeezing

Heat a large, wide-bottom soup pot over medium-high heat. Add the avocado oil, onion, and garlic and sauté for 3 to 5 minutes until the onion is soft but not browned. Stir in the tomatoes, cumin, and paprika. Cook for 2 minutes more.

Add the broth and cilantro and bring to a boil. Add the yucca and reduce to a simmer. Cook for about 20 minutes until the yucca is fork tender.

Now add the cubes of fresh tuna, and simmer for 10 minutes more until the tuna is just cooked through. Season with salt and pepper.

Spoon the soup into individual bowls and top with the Pickled Onions and Peppers, diced heirloom tomatoes (lightly salted), and a squeeze of fresh lime juice.

SEAFOOD CHOWDER

I absolutely love a good seafood chowder. Living in the Northeast now, I am partial to a solid clam and seafood chowder, red or white, but I will never lose my love for the fish stews of my childhood. My grandmother Netta in San Andrés, Colombia, used to make this stew with conch meat called Ron Don. My Mimi used to make a killer cioppino. And my mom makes a delicious white clam chowder with bacon. The challenge in making a healthy chowder is avoiding the traditional cream and potatoes. The cauliflower cream makes a fine substitute for heavy cream in most soup recipes, and arrowroot starch is a great thickening agent. I couldn't resist adding the bacon, but it can be omitted to keep the dish pescatarian.

Serves 4-6

- 4 slices nitrate-free natural bacon, diced into ¼-inch pieces (optional)
- 1 cup chopped yellow onion (½-inch dice)
- 1 tablespoon minced or grated garlic
- 1 ½ teaspoons sea salt
- ¾ teaspoon freshly cracked black pepper
- 2 cups cubed celery root (1-inch pieces) (about 2 medium pieces celery root)
- 1 cup peeled and cubed chayote squash
- (1-inch pieces) (about 1 medium squash)
- 1 cup peeled and cubed yucca root (1-inch pieces) (about half a root)
- 3 sprigs fresh thyme
- 8 ounces clam juice
- 1 cup water
- 1 cup canned coconut milk
- 1 pound chopped raw clams in juice
- 1 pound boneless white flaky but firm fish, such as halibut, cod, haddock, hake, or flounder, cubed into 2-inch pieces
- 1 cup Cauliflower Cream (see p. 64)
- 1 teaspoon arrowroot starch
- Additional sea salt and freshly cracked black pepper to taste

Garnishes:

- pork rinds
- chopped chives

Add the diced bacon to a large, wide-bottom soup pot. Set the pot over medium heat and cook the bacon for 2 to 3 minutes, rendering the fat out, until the bacon is lightly browned but not crispy. Using a slotted spoon, leaving the rendered bacon fat in the pot, carefully remove the bacon and set aside on a paper towel–lined plate. If not using bacon, you will need to add some fat to the pan to sauté the vegetables; about 2 tablespoons coconut oil will do.

Add the onion, garlic, salt, pepper, celery root, chayote, and yucca root to the pot. Sauté the vegetables in the bacon fat for 2 to 3 minutes. Add the thyme sprigs, clam juice, water, and coconut milk. Do not boil. Simmer for 15 minutes until the vegetables are tender.

Add the chopped clams, fish pieces, cooked bacon, and Cauliflower Cream. Sprinkle in the arrowroot starch, making sure to incorporate well into the broth. Simmer for an additional 5 minutes until fish and clams are just cooked through. Season to taste with salt and pepper.

Serve garnished with crumbled pork rinds and chopped chives.

CHILLED PAPAYA AND MELON SOUP

Chilled island soups are often enjoyed on those exceptionally hot days when the ocean breeze just isn't enough. You can make a chilled fruit soup with just about any fruit you want, but I use the combination of my favorite low-carb papaya and small amount of cantaloupe. When perfectly ripe, these two fruits create an out-of-this-world flavor combination. Paired with the cool herbs and just a touch of heat, this soup is sure to become a favorite in the summer months.

Serves 2

- 2 cups peeled, seeded, and cubed ripe papaya
- 1 cup peeled, seeded, and cubed ripe cantaloupe
- 1 cup coconut water
- 2 tablespoons lime juice
- 1 teaspoon minced fresh mint leaves, plus additional for garnish
- 1 teaspoon minced fresh cilantro leaves, plus additional for garnish
- ½ Scotch bonnet chile pepper, stemmed and seeded
- Flaked sea salt

Combine all ingredients in a high-powered blender and blend on high speed until smooth. For best results, chill for at least 3 hours before serving.

Pour into a chilled bowl and garnish with more fresh mint and cilantro and a small pinch of flake sea salt.

EASY CAULIFLOWER CREAM (HEAVY CREAM SUBSTITUE)

Most savory recipes calling for heavy cream can be substituted with this easy-to-make cauliflower cream, particularly sauces, soups, and purées. I don't recommend using in dessert prep as the water content can throw off the recipe, and the cauliflower flavor will come through without other savory flavors to mask it.

Makes 2 cups

- 1 pound cauliflower florets
- 1 cup water
- ¼ teaspoon sea salt

Place the cauliflower florets in a small pot with the water and salt. Cover and bring to a boil. Steam the cauliflower over high heat until fork tender, about 5 to 7 minutes.

Using a slotted spoon, transfer the cooked cauliflower to a blender, adding only enough of the cooking water to aid in blending (about half). Purée the cauliflower until completely smooth.

Transfer to an airtight container and refrigerate for up to 1 week until ready to use. Shake well before adding to any soups or sauces.

HOMEMADE CHILE OIL

Makes 2 cups

- ½ cup dried chile flakes
- ½ cup dried árbol chiles, chopped
- 1 ½ cups neutral oil, such as avocado or grapeseed oil
- ½ teaspoon garlic powder
- ½ teaspoon pink Himalayan salt

Combine the chile flakes and árbol chiles in a medium bowl.

Heat the oil in a small saucepan over medium heat until a thermometer reads 350°F, about 3 minutes.

Carefully pour the hot oil over the chiles. They will sizzle and steam. Be careful not to inhale the steam! Stir in the garlic powder and salt.

Allow the mixture to cool completely to room temperature before transferring to an airtight sanitized glass jar.

This oil can last up to 2 months at room temperature.

TOASTED PEPITAS

Pepitas are the inner part of a pumpkin seed. These toasted seeds have a great nutty, earthy flavor. They can be used in salads for crunch in place of croutons, as a soup topper, or eaten by themselves as a snack. They are also a great sub for nuts for anyone with a nut allergy.

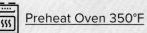 Preheat Oven 350°F

Makes 2 cups

- 2 cups raw pepitas (pumpkin seeds)
- 2 teaspoons avocado oil or extra-virgin olive oil
- 1 teaspoon fine sea salt

Preheat the oven to 350°F.

In a small bowl, combine pepitas, oil, and salt, stirring well so that the pepitas are completely and evenly coated.

Spread the pepitas on a baking sheet and bake for 10 to 15 minutes, stirring them halfway through cooking, until golden brown.

Remove from oven and transfer to a cool baking sheet. Allow pepitas to cool completely before transferring to an airtight container. Store at room temperature in your pantry for up to one month.

AVOCADO, TOMATILLA, AND CHARRED GREEN ONION GAZPACO

My husband and I got married in Tulum, Mexico, on the Yucatán. This dish is very reminiscent of all the flavors we love in the food there. We go back every year for our anniversary and eat until we can't eat anymore. Some of my favorite flavor profiles are born of the coastal Mayan cuisine of the Yucatán.

 Preheat Oven 375°F

Serves 4

- 2 pounds tomatillos, peeled
- 1 jalapeño pepper, stem removed
- 1 serrano chile pepper, stem removed
- 4 tablespoons avocado oil, divided
- 1 bunch green onions, trimmed
- Juice of 1 lime
- 1 ripe avocado, peeled and seeded
- ½ cup chopped fresh cilantro leaves
- ¼ cup toasted sliced almonds
- Sea salt to taste
- Splash of apple cider vinegar
- Pumpkin seed dip (optional)
- Fresh mint leaves, torn

Preheat the oven to 375°F.

Toss the tomatillos and whole chile peppers on a sheet tray with 1 tablespoon of the avocado oil. Roast for 20 to 30 minutes until the vegetables are beginning to brown in spots and softened.

Over an open flame (a burner on your stove will do), char the green onions whole, turning frequently, for about 4 to 5 minutes. Set aside.

In a blender, add the lime juice, avocado, remaining 3 tablespoons of avocado oil, and charred green onions first. Transfer the cooked tomatillos to the blender. Pulse and blend to start breaking up the vegetables, but do not purée.

Make a slit in each of the roasted chiles and gently remove the seeds. Add the seeded roasted chiles to the blender along with the almonds, a pinch of sea salt, and a splash of apple cider vinegar. Continue to pulse until the gazpacho is smooth and uniform but still has a slight bit of texture, about 3 to 4 minutes. Chill for at least 1 to 2 hours before serving.

Pour into chilled bowls and serve garnished with a spoonful of Mayan Hummus (pumpkin seed dip) (see recipe p. 82) and some fresh mint.

SMALL PLATES

One of the things I love about the cuisine of my heritage is that on most gathering tables you will find a beautiful spread of small plates and side dishes to kick off or accompany any meal. The beauty of preparing a small plate is that they can pack a punch with flavor, tantalizing the taste buds with intense layers of heat and acid. Because you usually eat one or two bites of each one, there is no worry about making them too heavy or too spicy. The variation of colors, flavors, and textures amplifies the mood for the rest of the meal. If you are entertaining, try mixing and matching a few appetizers along with a few side dishes and snacks plus a pitcher of cocktails for a beautiful and vibrant spread. One key tip for preparing small plates: always use the freshest ingredients possible.

- Baked Empanadas
- Colombian Empanada Hot Sauce
- Stuffed Yucca Island Patties
- Fire-Grilled Jerk Wings
- Crispy Oven-Baked Patacones
- Deviled Eggs
- Tuna Ceviche
- Grilled Cauliflower and Corn Esquites
- Pumpkin Seed Dip
- Hamachi Crudo with Agua Chile Verde
- Curried Eggplant Choka Dip
- Avocado Espuma
- Jerk Seasoning
- Mojo Sauce
- Passionfruit Chile Sauce (Salsa de Maracuya)

BAKED EMPANADAS

No matter what country you visit in Latin America or the Caribbean islands, you will find a version of these stuffed little hot pockets. In the islands they call them patties or turnovers and in Puerto Rico, pastelillos. The outer pocket can be made in a variety of different ways, some of which are a pastry and some that don't have any type of flour at all, like the following recipe for Stuffed Yucca Island Patties. Fillings vary from savory stewed meats and roasted vegetables to sweet custards or fruits. No matter what type of empanada you are making, you are sure to please the crowd. You can also make mini versions for parties. They freeze well once prepped, so you can just pull, thaw, and bake!

 Preheat Oven 375°F

Makes 4 to 6, or makes 10 large empanadas

- 1 very ripe plantain (the skin should be black)
- 1 cup cassava flour, sifted
- ¾ cup coconut flour
- ¼ cup arrowroot starch
- 1 teaspoon fine sea salt
- ¼ cup coconut shortening
- ¼ cup canned coconut milk
- 2 large organic eggs, divided
- 1 tablespoon water
- 2 ½ cups of prepared filling of your choice (I recommend Chicken Picadillo (p. 110) or Slow-Cooked Pork (p. 115), or 20 ounces by weight
- Avocado oil spray
- Colombian Empanada Hot Sauce (recipe follows)

Preheat the oven to 375°F.

Place the plantain, still in its peel, on a nonstick baking sheet and roast in the oven for 30 minutes.

Remove the baking sheet but leave the oven on.

Meanwhile, combine the cassava flour, coconut flour, arrowroot starch, and salt in a large bowl.

Peel the roasted plantain and mash into a paste. Chill slightly in the freezer for about 10 minutes.

Using a fork, cut the coconut shortening into the dry ingredients. Follow by cutting in the mashed plantain.

In a small bowl, whisk together the coconut milk and 1 egg, and pour into the flour mixture. Using your hands, work the dough into a ball. Mix it just long enough to combine; do not overwork. Divide the mixture into 10 portions.

In a small cup, whisk together the remaining egg and water to make an egg wash. Set aside.

To assemble the empanadas, flatten each ball of dough between parchment squares into a disk. Once flattened, the disks should be a uniform 5 inches or so in diameter. For each empanada, place 2 ounces (about ¼ cup) of filling off to one side of a disk, but not too close to the edge. Brush a ring of egg wash around the disk's outer edge. Using the parchment paper to assist you, fold the pouch closed into a crescent shape. Pinch together the edges in a decorative fashion, pressing the tines of a fork all along the seam.

Lightly grease the same nonstick baking sheet with avocado oil spray and place the empanadas on the sheet. Brush the tops with the remaining egg wash. Bake the empanadas for 40 minutes, or until the tops are golden brown and crisp. Serve with Colombian Empanada Hot Sauce.

COLOMBIAN EMPANADA HOT SAUCE

This tangy, spicy sauce can become addicting! You might want to double up batches because you will find yourself wanting to dip everything in it. Aside from empanadas, I love this sauce with crudités.

- ½ cup water
- ¼ cup apple cider vinegar
- 1 Scotch bonnet or habanero chile pepper, seeded and chopped
- 1 red Fresno chile pepper, seeded and chopped
- ¼ cup chopped white onion
- 1 clove garlic, peeled
- ½ teaspoon sea salt
- 1 teaspoon coconut sugar
- 1 tablespoon fresh lime juice
- 2 plum tomatoes, seeded and chopped
- ½ cup chopped fresh cilantro leaves

Combine all the ingredients except the tomatoes and cilantro in a blender and blend on high until smooth.

Add the chopped tomatoes and cilantro. Pulse two or three times to mix without puréeing. The hot sauce should have some texture to it. This hot sauce will keep for up to 2 weeks refrigerated.

STUFFED YUCCA ISLAND PATTIES

Island patties are like Caribbean hot pockets. They can really be stuffed with anything you want. The flavor of the crust is pretty neutral, so the filling flavors are what really shine through. Try adding cheese every once in a while for a special treat!

 Preheat Oven 375°F

Makes 4 to 6, or makes 10 large patties

- 2 pounds yucca, peeled and cut into large chunks
- 2 teaspoons fine sea salt
- 1 tablespoon arrowroot starch
- 2 ½ cups or 20 ounces of filling of your choosing (I recommend Easy Chicken Tinga (p. 113)
- Avocado oil
- Peruvian Green Sauce (p. 134)

For the yucca dough: Place the peeled yucca chunks in a large pot of cold salted water. Bring to a boil over medium-high heat, and cook for 20 minutes until the yucca is fork tender.

Drain the yuca, but do not rinse. Remove the stringy threads from the center of the roots and place them in a large bowl with the sea salt and arrowroot starch. Mash until completely smooth with the back of a spoon or a starch masher. Allow to cool slightly.

Divide the dough into 10 portions and roll into balls. Place each ball between 2 squares of parchment paper and flatten into uniform disks, about 4 to 5 inches in diameter.

For each empanada, place 2 ounces (about ¼ cup) of filling off to one side of a disk, but not too close to the edge. Using the parchment paper to assist you, fold the pouch closed into a crescent shape. Unlike the empanadas in the previous recipe, you don't need to create a decorative seal. Unlike flour empanadas, the edges will give way slightly during the cooking process.

Preheat the oven to 375°F.

Heat a heavy cast-iron skillet over medium-high heat. Add 2 tablespoons avocado oil to the pan. In batches, adding more avocado oil as needed, sear the patties for about 2 minutes on each side, until lightly browned. Transfer the patties carefully to a baking sheet and bake for another 10 minutes until cooked through and crisp.

Serve the fritters with delightful Peruvian Green Sauce.

FIRE-GRILLED JERK WINGS

There is something magical about cooking directly over an open flame, and fire pit cooking is quite common in many Latin countries. Using a grill basket makes it possible to roast all sorts of things without worrying about anything falling into the pit. The char is clean and smoky, crisping the skin if you are roasting in just the right proportions. I highly recommend getting yourself a grill basket and trying open-flame grilling right in your own barbecue. Just remove the grill grates and use natural charcoal bricks or wood that hasn't been soaked in lighter fluid (it will ruin the flavor of your food since the grill basket is placed right on top of the burning coals). Start grilling once the coals are bright red and hot and the flame has died down a bit. This will make for even cooking and charring and less blackening.

Makes 18 pieces

- 3 quarts water
- ¼ cup pink Himalayan salt
- 3 tablespoons coconut sugar
- 2 cloves garlic, peeled and smashed
- 1 tablespoon coriander seeds
- 1 bay leaf
- 9 organic whole chicken wings, broken down to flats and drumettes (or you can buy already prepped party wings)
- 4 tablespoons avocado oil
- 2 tablespoons Jerk Seasoning (p. 86)
- 1 recipe Passionfruit Chile Sauce (p. 87)
- 2 red Fresno chile peppers, seeded and sliced
- ½ bunch fresh cilantro leaves, cleaned and chopped

Combine the water, salt, coconut sugar, garlic, coriander, and bay leaf in a medium pot over medium-high heat. Bring to a boil and remove from heat. Allow to cool.

Place the wings in a large bowl and pour the brine over. Cover and refrigerate overnight.

Build the fire in a fire pit or grill.

Drain the wings and pat them dry to remove the excess brine.

Toss the wings with the avocado oil and Jerk Seasoning until they are thoroughly coated.

Place the wings in a single layer in a wide grill basket. Close the basket and grill directly over the hot coals, turning frequently, for about 20 minutes until cooked through. The wings will be charred in spots and crispy but not burned.

Serve wings with Passionfruit Chile Sauce, sliced red Fresno chiles, and chopped cilantro.

CRISPY OVEN-BAKED PATACONES

These crispy treats are usually fried, smashed, and then fried again and are called tostones in other parts of Latin America. This healthier baked version is just as delightful and goes well with a garlicky Mojo Sauce (p. 87). They also pair nicely with the Avocado and Scotch Bonnet Cashew Crema (p. 37). Patacones can be eaten as a snack or side dish and are often found on the dinner and breakfast table. They should be made fresh and eaten right away.

 Preheat Oven 425°F

Serves 4

- 4 large green plantains, peeled and sliced into ½-inch-thick slices
- Coconut oil spray
- 4 tablespoons coconut oil or avocado oil, divided
- 2 teaspoons sea salt, divided

Sauce for serving:

- Mojo Sauce (p. 87)
- Peruvian Green Sauce (p. 134) and/or Avocado and Scotch Bonnet Cashew Crema (p. 37)

Preheat the oven to 425°F.

Line a sheet pan with parchment paper and spray with coconut oil spray.

Toss the plantain slices with half of the oil and half of the sea salt, and spread them out on the prepared sheet pan.

Bake the plantains for 15 minutes, or until able to smash. Gently smash each plantain slice into a disk using the bottom of a heavy jar, cup, or any other round shatterproof object.

Brush the plantains with the remaining oil, and sprinkle them with the remaining salt. Toss to coat with oil on both sides.

Return the plantains to the oven and bake for another 15 minutes until crisp and golden. Serve right away with Mojo Sauce, Peruvian Green Sauce, or Avocado and Scotch Bonnet Cashew Crema.

DEVILED EGGS

Deviled eggs may be more of a staple of American southern cooking, but they will always be a go-to treat for me when I have company over. This version has a little kick, but you can omit the Scotch bonnet chile pepper if you prefer them not spicy. The key to excellent deviled eggs starts with the cooking process. This method can be used when making hard-boiled eggs in general and will ensure the yolks are perfectly bright yellow and cooked just right.

Makes 12 deviled eggs

- 8 large organic eggs
- Splash of apple cider vinegar
- Splash of olive oil
- 2–3 tablespoons mayonnaise made with olive oil or vegan mayonnaise
- 1 tablespoon Dijon mustard
- 2 tablespoons finely diced baby kosher dill pickles
- 2 tablespoons chopped capers plus 1 teaspoon of the brine
- 1 Scotch bonnet chile pepper, stemmed, seeded, and finely diced
- 2 dashes Tabasco sauce

Garnishes:

- Smoked paprika
- Crumbled pork rinds (about 3 table spoons)

Using a fine needle or pin, poke a tiny hole in each eggshell at the large end. Place the eggs in a medium pot and fill with just enough water to cover the eggs plus 1 inch. Add a splash of vinegar and a splash of olive oil to the water. This will help with peeling later.

Turn the heat to medium-high, starting a 15-minute timer right away from the moment the burner is turned on, and bring the eggs to a boil. Continue to cook until 10 minutes have passed on your kitchen timer. Remove the pan from the heat and allow the eggs to sit in the hot water for 5 more minutes, until the timer hits zero. The entire process from start to finish should be 15 minutes.

Using a slotted spoon, carefully remove the eggs from the hot water and place in a colander in the sink.

Under running cold water, quickly and carefully peel the eggs while they are still hot on the inside.

Cut 6 of the eggs in half lengthwise, wiping the knife off between each cut. Scoop the egg yolks out into a bowl. Add the other 2 whole boiled eggs to the bowl with the yolks. Set the cleaned out egg white halves upside down on a plate and place them in the refrigerator to chill.

Using a fork, mash the yolks and the two whole boiled eggs together to a pulp. Add the mayonnaise, Dijon mustard, pickles, capers, brine, scotch bonnet pepper, and Tabasco. Continue to whip the mixture with the fork until well combined and uniform.

Transfer the filling to a piping bag with either a small round or star tip, or to a Ziploc bag with a small hole (about a half inch in diameter) cut out of one corner. You can stop at this point until you are ready to serve. The filling can be refrigerated in the bag, and the egg whites covered with plastic wrap.

Remove the egg white halves from the refrigerator and flip them over. Pipe the filling into the egg whites in a decorative fashion. The filling should be mounded and taller than the height of the egg whites.

Sprinkle each egg white with a pinch of smoked paprika and some crumbled pork rinds.

TUNA CEVICHE

This vibrant bright pink and red ceviche is beautiful and refreshing. The fish must be super fresh and not "fishy." This dish should taste like the sea with dashes of tropical fruit and heat layered into every bite. Salt curing the fish ahead of time begins to "cook" the tuna slightly on the outside, adding a different texture on the palate. The dots of creamy Avocado Espuma here and there cut through the acid and the heat nicely.

Serves 4

- 1 pound ahi or big eye fresh tuna steaks, sushi grade
- 2 tablespoons flake sea salt

Red Tiger Water (Leche de Tigre):

- 1 prickly pear (cactus fruit), peeled and quartered
- 1 dragon fruit, peeled and quartered
- 1 English cucumber, peeled and cut into chunks
- 1 serrano chile pepper, stem removed
- 1 cup coconut water
- 1 cup freshly squeezed pink grapefruit juice
- ¼ cup freshly squeezed lime juice
- Sea salt to taste
- 3 radishes, sliced and cut into match sticks
- 2 tablespoons fresh pomegranate seeds
- 2 tablespoons pickled onions and peppers (p. 46)
- 1 additional serrano chile pepper, stemmed, seeded, and shaved paper thin
- Fresh cilantro sprigs
- Fresh opal basil leaves (or young regular basil will work too)
- Fresh mint leaves
- Avocado Espuma (p. 86) (optional)
- Olive oil for drizzling
- Zest of 1 lime

Trim and clean off all of the dark-red blood line from the tuna and cut the tuna steaks into rectangular logs, about 2 inches wide.

Sprinkle the tuna logs all over with the flake sea salt. Press gently to ensure the salt adheres to the flesh. Refrigerate the salted tuna steaks for 40 to 45 minutes to lightly cure.

In the meantime, make the red leche de tigre: Place the prickly pear, dragon fruit, cucumber, 1 serrano chile, coconut water, grapefruit juice, and lime juice in a blender. Blend on high until uniform and as smooth as possible. Season lightly with salt.

Strain the leche de tigre through a fine mesh strainer, pressing gently on the pulp to get as much liquid out of it as possible. Refrigerate to chill.

Pull the salted tuna from the refrigerator and wipe gently with damp paper towels to remove the bulk of the salt cure. Using a very sharp knife, slice the tuna against the grain into ¼-inch-thick slices. Keep your knife at a 45-degree angle, making clean, one-motion cuts. Avoid sawing the tuna.

In a small bowl, toss the tuna slices with a few spoonfuls of the leche de tigre and allow to sit for 2 to 3 minutes before plating.

Divide the remaining leche de tigre among 4 shallow bowls. Divide and arrange the marinated slices of tuna down the center or around the outer edge of one side of the bowl.

Next, arrange the radish matchsticks along the top of the tuna in a decorative alternating fashion. Follow with pomegranate seeds, Pickled Onions and Peppers, then 4 or 5 slices of the remaining serrano chile.

Finish your design with the fresh herbs, a few dots of Avocado Espuma, and a drizzle of olive oil. Grate some fresh lime zest all over the dish with a Microplane or fine grater.

GRILLED CAULIFLOWER AND CORN ESQUITES

Street corn is a weakness of mine—I can't help but order it every time I'm eating Mexican cuisine. Corn isn't that good for you, so when I do eat it, it has to be worth it. Blending the charred corn with roasted cauliflower cuts the carbs while preserving the sweetness of the corn.

 Preheat Oven 400°F

Serves 4

The Vegetables:

- 1 small head cauliflower, cut into florets
- 2 tablespoons coconut or avocado oil
- ½ teaspoon salt
- ½ teaspoon chile de árbol powder
- 2 ears fresh corn, husked
- 1 tablespoon coconut or avocado oil

Chile Cream Sauce:

- ¼ cup mayonnaise made with olive oil or vegan mayo
- ¼ cup Plain Cashew Crema (p. 37)
- ½ teaspoon chile de árbol powder
- 1 teaspoon adobo sauce (from canned chipotle chiles)
- 1 clove garlic
- 1 tablespoon lime juice
- 1 teaspoon minced fresh dill
- ¼ teaspoon sea salt

For Assembling:

- Crumbled cotija cheese
- Chopped fresh cilantro
- Lime wedges

Preheat the oven to 400°F.

Prepare the vegetables: On a baking sheet, toss the cauliflower florets with the 2 tablespoons coconut oil, ½ teaspoon salt, and ½ teaspoon chili powder. Spread the florets out evenly. Bake the cauliflower for 35 to 40 minutes until tender and beginning to char and caramelize in spots. Remove the cauliflower from the oven and allow to cool while preparing the corn. Once cool, chop cauliflower into "kernels" the same size as the corn. Transfer to a medium bowl.

While the vegetables are baking, prepare the Chile Cream Sauce.

Combine mayo, Cashew Crema, chile de árbol powder, adobo sauce, garlic, lime juice, dill, and salt in a blender. Blend on high speed until smooth. Scoop out into a bowl and set aside.

Rub the corn cobs all over with just enough oil to coat. Heat a cast-iron grill pan over medium-high heat. Grill the corn cobs, turning frequently, until the corn kernels are cooked and charred slightly on the outside. Remove the corn from the pan and allow to cool. Once cool, cut the corn kernels off the cob and mix them with the cauliflower.

Heat a medium-size sauté pan over medium-high heat. Add a teaspoon of avocado oil to the pan. Add the cauliflower and corn kernel mix and sauté for 2 to 3 minutes until heated through. Add half the Chile Cream Sauce to the pan and toss a few times, just enough to incorporate. Immediately remove from heat and spoon the mix onto a serving platter.

Drizzle the remaining Chile Cream Sauce over the top of the cauliflower and corn in a zigzag pattern. Sprinkle with cotija cheese (optional), and garnish with freshly chopped cilantro.

Surround the platter with lime wedges for squeezing over the top.

PUMPKIN SEED DIP

I love regular hummus, but chickpeas, while they contain a lot of fiber, also have a lot of carbs. This dip eats like a hummus and has been made in Mayan cultures for centuries. Traditionally it was made in a molcajete (mortar and pestle), ground by hand until smooth. But the task is easier—and the resulting texture is smoother—using a food processor. You can serve this dip with crisp cut crudités or grilled flatbread.

 Preheat Oven 400°F

Serves 4

- 1 medium white onion, peeled and halved
- 1 jalapeño pepper, stemmed but whole
- 2 medium tomatillos, peeled
- 1 plum tomato
- 4 cloves garlic, peeled
- 1 cup hulled raw pumpkin seeds
- ¼ cup shelled raw sunflower seeds
- 3 tablespoons avocado oil
- Juice and zest from 1 orange
- Juice and zest from 1 lime
- ¼ cup chopped fresh cilantro leaves
- ¼ cup chopped fresh mint leaves
- Sea salt to taste
- Extra-virgin olive oil (optional)
- Chili powder (optional)

Preheat the oven to 400°F.

Place the onion, jalapeño, tomatillos, plum tomato, and garlic cloves on a baking sheet and roast dry in the oven until fork tender and charred, about 30 to 40 minutes.

Heat a large sauté pan over medium heat. Add the pumpkin seeds and sunflower seeds to the dry pan and toast, tossing frequently, until golden and fragrant, about 5 to 7 minutes.

Transfer the seeds to a food processor and set aside.

In the same sauté pan over medium heat, add the avocado oil. Slide the roasted vegetables from the oven into the pan and cook for about 5 minutes until soft and broken down. Add this mixture to the food processor with the toasted seeds. Allow to cool until warm to the touch, about 10 to 15 minutes.

Add the orange juice and zest, lime juice and zest, cilantro, and mint. Add a splash of cool water and begin to blend until puréed and nearly smooth. Season with sea salt to taste and pulse 2 or 3 times more.

Transfer the dip to a bowl. Drizzle with olive oil and a pinch of chili powder before serving if you'd like.

HAMACHI CRUDO with AGUACHILE VERDE

Over the years I have enjoyed gradually introducing spirits into my food, particularly rum in my Caribbean cooking and tequila or mezcal into my Latin dishes. Here, the introduction of mezcal into the Aguachile adds a layer of smoky bitterness. If you are not a fan of mezcal (it's not for everyone), try using a clean añejo tequila of high quality. Most important, make aguachile as close to when you are going to serve it as possible—never the day before. It's quick and easy and worth it.

Serves 4

- 1 ½ pounds hamachi fillets, skinned and cut into 2-inch wide logs

Aguachile:

- 1 small English cucumber, peeled and cut into chunks
- 1 ½ ounces good-quality mezcal
- 2 small tomatillos, husked and cut into chunks
- 1 serrano chile pepper, stemmed and chopped
- 1 teaspoon honey or agave
- ¼ cup freshly squeezed lime juice
- ¼ cup coconut water
- ¼ cup chopped fresh cilantro leaves
- Sea salt to taste

For Assembling:

- Flake sea salt
- 4 shishito peppers
- 1 small white onion, peeled and shaved into thin slices
- 1 small avocado, peeled, seeded, and cubed
- ¼ cup pomegranate seeds

Thinly slice the hamachi on a bias, about ⅛ of an inch thick. Arrange on a large round or oval platter. Cover and place in freezer to chill while preparing the aguachile, but not for more than 15 to 20 minutes. Transfer to the refrigerator if you are not ready to serve yet.

Make the aguachile: In a blender, combine the cucumber, mezcal, tomatillos, serrano chile, honey, lime juice, coconut water, and cilantro. Blend for 30 to 45 seconds. Strain through a fine strainer into a bowl and discard the solids. Add salt to taste, about ½ teaspoon, to the aguachile liquid. Set aside.

Over an open flame (a stove burner will do), char the shishito peppers, turning frequently, for about 1 to 2 minutes. Quickly slice into ⅓-inch rings.

Remove the fish platter from the freezer or refrigerator and pour the aguachile over it—enough to gorgeously coat the fish, but not enough that you can't see the fish.

Sprinkle all over with a few pinches of flake salt. Follow with the charred shishito rings, shaved onion, avocado cubes, and finally, the fresh pomegranate seeds.

CURRIED EGGPLANT CHOKA DIP

This Caribbean dip is similar to what you would call eggplant caviar stateside. This choka will come out best if you are able to roast the eggplant over an open flame, but oven roasting will work as well. The open flame adds a nice smoky flavor.

 Preheat Oven 450°F

Serves 4

- 2 medium eggplants, stems removed
- 4 tablespoons extra-virgin olive oil or avocado oil, divided
- 1 Scotch bonnet chile pepper
- 2 cloves garlic, whole and peeled
- 3 green onions, trimmed and sliced thin, white and green parts
- ½ teaspoon curry powder
- ¼ teaspoon ground cumin
- Squeeze of fresh lime juice
- Sea salt to taste
- 2 cloves garlic, minced

If oven roasting, preheat the oven to 450°F. If using an open-flame grill, clean the grill grates and preheat to 400°F.

Rub the eggplants all over with 2 tablespoons olive oil. Using a sharp paring knife, make a few slits all over the eggplant. If baking, place on a baking sheet and roast for 45 minutes. If grilling, place on the grate and turn every 15 minutes. Add the Scotch bonnet chile pepper and the whole garlic cloves to the oven or grill for the last 10 minutes.

Remove the eggplants, pepper, and garlic from the heat.

In a mortar and pestle or a food processor, place the Scotch bonnet chile pepper and the garlic cloves. Grind into a paste.

Cut the eggplants open and scoop out the soft roasted pulp and add it to the pepper and garlic paste. Add the sliced green onions, curry powder, and cumin, along with a squeeze of fresh lime juice and 1 tablespoon olive oil. Season with salt and set aside.

In a small sauté pan, heat the remaining tablespoon of olive oil and add the minced garlic. Stirring constantly, pan roast the minced garlic until it turns golden brown and crispy. Immediately scrape the roasted garlic along with the cooking oil into the dip and stir to stop the cooking.

Serve with fresh cut crudités or low-carb flatbread.

AVOCADO ESPUMA

This satiny condiment tastes so decadent but is deceivingly good for you. I like to smear it on lettuce leaves when making lettuce cups, or on a slice of low-carb bread when making a sandwich. It can also be drizzled on tacos or dotted on plates of ceviche. Treat it like a mayo of sorts.

Makes 1 cup

- 1 ripe avocado
- ½ cup Cashew Crema (p. 37)
- 2 tablespoons canned coconut milk
- Juice and zest of 1 lime
- ¼ teaspoon sea salt

Combine all ingredients in a blender and blend until completely smooth. Scrape down and stir two or three times at intervals. Transfer to a piping bag or a Ziploc bag with a small hole cut off one of the corners for easy drizzling. Alternatively it can be transferred and stored in a small bowl until ready to use.

JERK SEASONING

Who doesn't love a good Jamaican jerk seasoning? Traditionally, jerk seasoning is mostly used with chicken, but don't be afraid to try rubbing it on fish or shrimp too! I like making my own because the flavors are so much more vibrant. Store-bought jerk seasoning could have been made months ago, and spices tend to lose their potency after a while. I tend to go through spices quickly, so most of the spices used are fresh.

Makes ½ cup

- 1 teaspoon fine sea salt
- 1 teaspoon fresh finely ground black pepper
- 2 tablespoons coconut sugar
- 2 tablespoons onion powder
- 1 tablespoon garlic powder
- 1 tablespoon cayenne pepper
- 2 teaspoons smoked or sweet paprika
- 1 teaspoon ground allspice
- ½ teaspoon ground cinnamon
- ¼ teaspoon ground cloves
- 1 teaspoon red chile flakes
- ½ teaspoon ground cumin
- 1 teaspoon dried thyme

Mix all ingredients together in a bowl. Store in an airtight spice jar in the pantry. Use within 3 months.

MOJO SAUCE

Mojo is a term used widely for a lot of different variations of chile sauce, but this particular Cuban-style mojo refers to a sauce made with sour citrus, lots of garlic, herbs, and oil. This sauce is enjoyed most often with crispy yucca or plantains.

Makes 1 ½ cups

- ½ cup freshly squeezed orange juice
- ¼ cup freshly squeezed lime juice
- 5 cloves garlic
- 2 green onions, both greens and whites used, trimmed and chopped roughly
- ¼ teaspoon ground cumin
- ¼ teaspoon ground coriander
- 1 teaspoon dried oregano
- 1 teaspoon sea salt
- ¼ teaspoon freshly cracked black pepper
- ¼ cup fresh cilantro leaves
- ¼ cup extra-virgin olive oil

Combine all ingredients in a blender or food processor. Pulse until the mixture is uniform and creamy, but still has a bit of texture. Serve right away, or refrigerate and store for up to 2 days. After 2 days' time, you can still use this mojo for up to 1 week as a marinade for chicken or pork before cooking.

PASSIONFRUIT CHILE SAUCE (SALSA DE MARACUYA)

Makes 2 cups

- 4 aji amarillo chile peppers, stemmed
- 1 Scotch bonnet chile pepper, stemmed and seeded
- ½ cup fresh passionfruit pulp (about 2 passionfruit)
- ½ cup freshly squeezed orange juice (about 1 large orange), plus zest
- 2 tablespoons freshly squeezed lime juice (about 1 lime)
- 1 tablespoon coconut sugar or agave nectar
- ¼ cup Valentina hot sauce
- ¼ cup avocado oil
- Sea salt and freshly cracked black pepper to taste

Heat a pot of salted water over medium-high heat and bring to a boil. Blanch the peppers for about 10 minutes. Remove the peppers and shock them in a bowl of ice water to stop the cooking and retain their bright colors. Place the cooked peppers in a blender and add the remaining ingredients except the avocado oil, salt, and black pepper. Blend until completely smooth.

Turn the blender to low and slowly drizzle in the avocado oil.

Season with salt and pepper to taste.

SALADS

I have always been a salad lover. Growing up in a "granola town" like Santa Cruz, I developed a bond for this genre of cuisine at a very early age. My passion for salads grew even stronger when I went to work at an organic farm in Watsonville at age fourteen. Being part of the cycle of farming fresh lettuces and vegetables does something to the senses. For me, salads are all about textures and layers of flavor. The combinations are infinite. One thing is certain: any one of these salads will transport you to the seaside somewhere.

- Butter Lettuce Salad
- Cho Cho and Jicama Salad
- Island Green Salad
- Cucumber and Papaya Salad
- Avocado and Heirloom Tomato Salad
- Warm Octopus Salad
- Avocado Goddess Dressing
- Cumin Vinaigrette
- Simple Lime Vinaigrette
- Herbed Caper and Olive Salsa
- Papaya Vinaigrette
- Quick Pan-Roasted and Salted Sunflower Seeds

BUTTER LETTUCE SALAD

With only four elements smothered in this creamy vibrant dressing, less is more with this salad. Adding avocado to the green goddess dressing instead of the classic combo of butter lettuce topped with slices of avocado really allows you to get the crunch from the leaves and radishes while still getting that hint of creamy avocado flavor and texture. Finish with a few flakes of sea salt and a crack of fresh black pepper, and you are golden.

Serves 4

- 2 heads butter lettuce, cored
- 1 cup Avocado Goddess Dressing (p. 100)
- 8 to 10 assorted colored radishes, shaved thin to ⅛ inch and soaked in ice water for at least 15 minutes
- ¼ cup pomegranate seeds (about half a fresh pomegranate)
- ¼ cup hulled roasted salted sunflower seeds
- Flake salt and freshly cracked black pepper (optional)

Wash the butter lettuce leaves in cold water and allow to dry on a baking sheet lined with paper towels while prepping the dressing and other ingredients, so that the lettuce crisps up.

Divide half of the leaves among 4 plates. Spoon a few tablespoons of the dressing over the first layer of lettuce. Divide the remaining lettuce among the 4 plates, and spoon the remaining dressing over the top of the leaves.

Sprinkle the radishes all over the salads.

Next, sprinkle the salads with pomegranate seeds.

Lastly, finish with sunflower seeds.

I highly recommend finishing the salad with some flake salt and freshly cracked black pepper.

CHO CHO AND JICAMA SALAD

By now you have surely noticed that cho cho, the Caribbean nickname for chayote, has made a few appearances in this book, and it's for good reason. This squash is so incredibly versatile that it can easily be used in sweet and savory applications. As you have already seen before, when used in soups, it eats like a potato. When baked with sweetener, as you will find in the dessert section, it eats like an apple. But here in this salad, it eats like a squash, which it is. A quick blanch and shock of the cho cho takes away some of the raw bite, while leaving the firm texture of a zucchini cooked al dente. In this salad, the flavors of the earthy jicama meshed with the tangy cumin vinaigrette and the briny Spanish green olives works really nicely together. I like the spicy bite of arugula, but you can use baby mixed greens instead if you prefer.

Serves 4

- 2 cups peeled and cubed chayote squash (in 1-inch cubes—about 2 small chayote)
- 1 cup peeled, halved, and sliced jicama (in ⅛-inch slices)
- ¼ cup Cumin Vinaigrette (p. 100) (divided)
- Pinch of sea salt
- ¼ cup fresh cilantro leaves
- ¼ cup fresh mint leaves
- ¼ cup Toasted Pepitas (p. 65), divided
- ¼ cup shaved red onion (paper thin)
- 2 cups wild arugula
- ¼ cup sliced green Spanish olives
- Freshly cracked black pepper

Bring a pot of generously salted water to a boil over medium-high heat and prepare a bowl of ice water. Line a baking sheet with a rack.

Add the chayote to the boiling water and boil for about 2 to 3 minutes. Do not overcook. Using a slotted spoon to not damage the flesh, transfer the blanched cho cho to the ice bath. Dunk it quickly in and out of the ice bath twice. Place the squash on the baking sheet rack to cool. It's important not to leave the squash cooling in the ice water or it will get water logged. The rack helps to allow excess water to drain.

In a wooden salad bowl, toss the cooked squash with the jicama and 2 tablespoons of Cumin Vinaigrette. Add a pinch of salt and allow to marinate for 5 to 10 minutes.

Add the fresh cilantro, mint, half of the pepitas, red onion, arugula, and olives to the bowl. Add the remaining dressing and gently mix.

Sprinkle with remaining pepitas and finish with freshly cracked black pepper.

ISLAND GREEN SALAD

Any sort of greens can be used for this salad. I like to have a nice contrast of crunch, spice, and grassy flavor. The torn herbs give another dimension of flavor but can be omitted if you prefer to just use a baby spring mix. Try throwing in some sprouting greens too.

Serves 4

- 16 ounces mixed washed greens such as arugula, baby kale, baby gems, and red leaf

Try Adding:

- Hoja santa leaves, stems removed and torn
- Fresh mint leaves torn
- Fresh cilantro leaves
- Fresh purple basil leaves
- Sunflower sprouts

Remainder of the Salad:

- ¼ cup shaved red onion
- 1 English cucumber, peeled, seeded, and sliced
- ¼ cup toasted salted guara almonds, divided
- ¼ cup Papaya Vinaigrette (p. 102)
- Sea salt and freshly cracked black pepper to taste
- Crumbled farmers cheese (optional)

Place the clean mixed greens and any herbs or sprouts in a wooden salad bowl. Add the onion, cucumber, half the almonds, and the Papaya Vinaigrette. Add a pinch of salt and cracked black pepper and gently toss to combine. Check again for seasoning.

Sprinkle the remaining almonds over the top of the salad and serve. Add some crumbled farmers cheese if you like.

CUCUMBER AND PAPAYA SALAD

Light and refreshing, this is a summertime favorite. If you aren't a papaya fan, this salad does nicely with juicy ripe pineapple or mango. Keep in mind, though, those fruits will double the sugar content, so if you are going to swap, save it for a cheat day on the beach and pack this salad on ice to enjoy with an ice-cold *cerveza*.

Serves 4

- 2 large English cucumbers, peeled, halved, seeded, and sliced ¼ inch thick
- 1 large ripe orange papaya, peeled, seeded, and diced into 1-inch cubes
- ½ medium red onion sliced thin
- ¼ cup fresh mint leaves, torn
- ¼ cup fresh cilantro leaves, torn
- ¼ cup fresh flat-leaf parsley, torn
- 1 tablespoon shaved serrano chiles
- Queso fresco cubes (optional)
- ¼ cup Lime Vinaigrette (p. 101)
- Sea salt and freshly cracked black pepper to taste

Combine all ingredients except salt and pepper in a large bowl and gently toss to combine. Season to taste with salt and pepper.

AVOCADO and HEIRLOOM TOMATO SALAD

On a trip to Ibiza, Spain, I remember eating the most amazing salad of perfectly ripe tomatoes, white onions, sea salt, garlic, and olive oil. It was arguably the best tomato salad I've ever had. I have had similar experiences on several of my trips to Italy during the season when the tomatoes are just right, served with a spicy, grassy, unfiltered olive oil. A similar joy is eating an absolutely perfect avocado with fresh lime and sea salt. Many a table in Latin and Caribbean households will serve a simple platter of avocados like this. When heirloom tomatoes aren't in season, you can swap in perfectly ripe peaches. This salad is best served at room temperature, except for the optional addition of dollops of cold cottage cheese.

Serves 4

- 2 large perfectly ripe Hass avocados, peeled, seeded, and cut in ¼-inch-thick slices, at room temperature
- 2 large ripe heirloom tomatoes, in season, at room temperature
- 1 clove garlic, minced or finely grated
- 2 pinches flake sea salt
- Squeeze of fresh lime juice
- 2 tablespoons very high quality extra-virgin olive oil
- ¼ cup cottage cheese
- 3 tablespoons Herbed Caper and Olive Salsa (p. 101)
- Freshly cracked black pepper

Place the avocados in a wooden salad bowl and set aside. Halve the tomatoes and place them on the cutting board cut-side down. Cut each half into 4 wedges. Add the tomato wedges to the salad bowl.

Add the garlic to the avocados and tomatoes, along with the flake salt, a squeeze of fresh lime juice, and the olive oil. Very gently, using your fingertips, toss the fruits until they are coated. It's best not to use tongs or any tool for this; they will damage the avocados and tomatoes. Allow the avocados and tomatoes to marinate at room temperature for 20 minutes.

On a decorative platter, arrange the avocado slices in a mosaiclike pattern. Next arrange the tomato wedges in the empty spaces. Next, spoon dollops of cottage cheese in the remaining empty spaces on the plate. Drizzle the leftover juices from the salad bowl over some of the tomatoes. Finally, spoon the Herbed Caper and Olive Salsa in a zigzag pattern across the platter, making sure there is some touching at least half of the fruits and cheese. Crack fresh pepper across the platter.

WARM OCTOPUS SALAD

The Caribbean Sea is full of these creatures, so it's no surprise that you will find them on pretty much any coastal menu. Although it can be intimidating working with a whole octopus, it's actually quite simple. The secret is the layers of cooking, manipulating the texture. Here we boil first, grill next, and then marinate/cure. The end result is a melt-in-your-mouth texture coupled with the crunch of a charred exterior. There is almost nothing worse than chewy, fishy, undercooked, or ill-prepared octopus. Take the time to nail this. You can also prepare just the tentacles if you are more comfortable with them, and skip dealing with the head. This recipe is one of those few times I will break open a sugary pineapple—in moderation, of course.

Serves 4

Octopus:

- 2 bay leaves
- 3 parsley stalks
- 3 sprigs thyme
- 1 lemon, halved
- Sea salt
- 1 (2 ½ pound) octopus, or 2 pounds tentacles only
- Coconut oil for grilling

Dressing:

- 1 tablespoon coriander seeds, dry toasted and ground fine
- 1 poblano chile pepper, roasted, peeled, and seeded
- 1 clove garlic
- 1 small shallot, minced
- 1 teaspoon honey or agave
- 2 tablespoons freshly squeezed lime juice
- ½ cup extra-virgin olive oil or avocado oil
- ¼ teaspoon sea salt

Salad:

- ½ ripe pineapple, peeled, cored, and diced into ¼ inch pieces
- 1 Scotch bonnet or habanero pepper, seeded and minced
- 2 red Fresno chile peppers, sliced into ⅛-inch rings
- 1 small white onion, peeled and very thinly shaved
- ¼ cup fresh cilantro leaves
- 2 cups baby arugula

Garnish:

- fresh lime wedges

Prepare the octopus: Fill a large pot with water, enough to cover the octopus when added. Add the bay leaves, parsley stalks, thyme sprigs, lemon halves, and a generous amount of salt. Bring to a boil and allow to cook for ten minutes to allow the flavors to blend.

Gently pound the tentacles of the octopus with the smooth side of a mallet or any smooth, heavy object. This will tenderize the meat.

Holding the octopus by its head, dunk the body in and out of the water 2 or 3 times for about 5 to 10 seconds each time. Then carefully submerge the octopus into the water. Cook for 45 minutes to 1 hour, until the tentacles are tender. You should be able to easily insert a fork into the octopus.

Immediately remove from the cooking liquid and dunk the octopus into ice water 4 to 5 times.

Cut the tentacles off the body and place in a bowl covered tightly with plastic wrap. Refrigerate while preparing the dressing and salad ingredients.

Preheat your grill to 400°F, or a cast-iron grill pan on your stove.

Make the dressing: Combine the coriander, poblano, garlic, shallot, honey, lime juice, oil, and salt in a blender. Pulse until combined and uniform.

Toss the octopus with coconut oil and 2 tablespoons of prepared dressing to marinate. Grill the octopus for about 4 to 5 minutes on each side, until crispy.

While the octopus is grilling, combine all of the salad ingredients except the arugula in a salad bowl. Add 1 to 2 tablespoons of dressing and toss to combine.

On a platter, arrange the baby arugula. Sprinkle the salad mixture over the bed of arugula.

Once the octopus is crispy, remove from the grill and immediately slice on a bias into ¼-inch-thick slices. Arrange the warm octopus on top of the salad bed, and spoon a generous amount of the coriander dressing all over the top. Garnish the platter with lime wedges all around.

Tip: The octopus head can be discarded if you aren't comfortable eating it, but when thinly sliced, can be sautéed with garlic and olive oil and then added to the salad along with the tentacles. It adds a nice calamari-like texture to the salad.

AVOCADO GODDESS DRESSING

Green goddess dressing is a salad dressing most often made with lots of mayonnaise, herbs, and citrus. The use of avocado allows for the same creaminess without the use of mayo. We are able to add just a small amount of Cashew Crema as well to add to the silky texture. This dressing is also great as a dip.

Makes 1 ½ cups

- Juice of 3 limes
- ¼ cup chopped fresh cilantro leaves
- 2 tablespoons chopped fresh parsley leaves
- 2 tablespoons chopped fresh chives
- 1 teaspoon minced garlic
- 1 teaspoon apple cider vinegar
- 1 teaspoon coconut sugar
- ¼ cup extra-virgin olive oil
- 1 large ripe avocado (the fresher, the better)
- ¼ cup homemade Cashew Crema (p. 37)
- Sea salt and freshly cracked black pepper to taste

Combine all ingredients in a high-powered blender and blend on high until completely smooth and uniform. Scrape down the sides periodically to make sure all ingredients are incorporated.

CUMIN VINAIGRETTE

Cumin is very warm and earthy, almost herbal with a hint of spice. The combination of the cumin and the citrus juices make for a pungent vibrant dressing that can stand up to heartier ingredients rather than simple lettuce salads.

Makes 1 cup

- 1 teaspoon ground cumin
- ½ teaspoon Dijon mustard
- ¼ cup freshly squeezed lime juice
- ¼ cup freshly squeezed orange juice
- 1 teaspoon honey
- ¾ cup avocado oil
- Sea salt and freshly cracked black pepper to taste

Whisk together the cumin, mustard, citrus juices, and honey in a small bowl. Slowly drizzle in the avocado oil, while whisking, to emulsify. Season with salt and pepper.

SIMPLE LIME VINAIGRETTE

This is a very light go-to everyday vinaigrette. I love this on fruit salads and tender baby lettuces.

Makes ½ cup

- Juice of 2 limes (about ¼ cup)
- 1 teaspoon Dijon mustard
- 1 teaspoon coconut sugar
- 1 teaspoon sea salt
- ¼ cup avocado oil

Combine all ingredients in a small clean glass jar with lid. Shake vigorously for 30 seconds. Refrigerate until ready to use. This dressing is best when made fresh, so it should not be stored for more than 2 to 3 days.

HERBED CAPER AND OLIVE SALSA

This salsa is marvelous with Avocado and Heirloom Tomato Salad (p. 103), but it has many other applications as well. Try it with Crispy Chicken Thighs (p. 115) or a piece of grilled swordfish.

Makes 2 cups

- ½ cup capers plus 1 tablespoon brine
- ½ cup Spanish green olives, sliced, plus 1 tablespoon brine
- ½ cup chopped fresh cilantro leaves
- ¼ cup chopped fresh parsley leaves
- 1 teaspoon Mexican oregano
- 1 tablespoon finely chopped fresh thyme leaves
- 1 serrano chile, stemmed, seeded, and finely diced
- ¼ teaspoon salt
- ¼ teaspoon ground cumin
- ¼ teaspoon red pepper flakes
- ¼ cup extra-virgin olive oil
- 1 tablespoon freshly squeezed lime juice

Place all the ingredients except the two brines and the lime juice into a blender. Pulse gently just to combine and lightly chop, but do not purée. Transfer the mixture to a bowl. Stir in the caper brine, olive brine, and lime juice. Allow the salsa to sit for 30 minutes before using. You can refrigerate until ready to use, but let it come to room temperature before serving.

PAPAYA VINAIGRETTE

The papaya in this dressing isn't overpowering. It just adds a hint of subtle fruity flavor and natural sweetness. Often, a dressing like this is made with mango or passionfruit, but the papaya adds a more subtle nuance and, of course, contains less sugar and carbs.

Makes 1 cup

- ½ cup chopped fresh ripe papaya
- ¼ cup freshly squeezed lime juice
- 1 tablespoon apple cider vinegar
- 1 tablespoon coconut sugar
- 1 teaspoon Dijon mustard
- ½ teaspoon pink Himalayan salt
- 1 pinch ground cloves
- ½ cup extra-virgin olive oil

In a blender, add all ingredients except the olive oil. Blend on high for 1 minute. Turn the blender speed down to low. Slowly drizzle in the olive oil, with the blender running, until fully combined and emulsified. Adjust seasoning with more salt or sugar if needed.

QUICK PAN-ROASTED AND SALTED SUNFLOWER SEEDS

Similar to pepitas (pumpkin seeds), toasted sunflower seeds are a nice substitute for croutons in a salad for crunch. They also make a great snack on their own.

Makes 2 cups

- 2 cups shelled raw sunflower seeds
- 1 tablespoon avocado oil
- 1 teaspoon fine sea salt

Place the sunflower seeds in a medium skillet and heat over medium heat. Stirring frequently, toast the sunflower seeds for about 5 to 7 minutes, until lightly browned and aromatic.

Stir in the avocado oil and sea salt and heat for 2 minutes more.

Remove the seeds from the skillet and spread onto a baking sheet to cool.

Allow to cool completely before transferring to an airtight container. Store at room temperature for up to 1 month.

LARGE PLATES AND SIDES

Most Latin and Caribbean main dishes are rich in protein and carbs, and for most families, those recipes define generations, passed on from mothers and fathers to their sons and daughters. These are the plates that transport us back in time with the first bite and remind us of surrounding the dinner table as children. Reworking these recipes has been important to me so that I pass on healthier versions of my beloved favorites to my own children. The key was replacing processed seasonings, sugar-laden canned tomato products, and carb-heavy starches with healthy choices. I have combined the main plates and sides in one section because I believe these are good pairings, but any of the sides can be made as stand-alone plates as well.

- Crispy Chicken Thighs
- Perfect Chicken Breast
- Almost Burned Butter Celeriac Root Purée
- Chicken Picadillo
- Large Cilantro Cauliflower Coconut Rice
- Easy Chicken Tinga (Tacos with Jicama Shells)
- Slow-Cooked Pork
- All-Day Costillas (Ribs)
- Braised Oxtails, Cuban Style
- Pumpkin Fufu
- Churrasco with Chimichurri
- Coconut Creamed Greens
- Mackerel Vera Cruz Style
- Shrimp and "Grits"
- Creamed Yucca
- Roasted Spaghetti Squash
- Whole Grilled Fish
- Curried Green Plantains and Jackfruit
- Avocado-Papaya Salsa
- Cashew and Chile de árbol Salsa Macha
- Chimichurri Sauce
- Crispy Onion, Garlic, and Chile Oil
- Peruvian Green Sauce (Aji Verde)
- Pickled Cucumbers and Green Papaya

CRISPY CHICKEN THIGHS

One thing is certain: any night that I cook chicken at my house is a happy night. What I love about cooking chicken thighs is that they are so forgiving and actually get juicier and more tender the longer you cook them. That's why I use them for my Chicken Tinga (p. 113) later instead of breasts. For these crispy-skin chicken thighs, low and slow is the name of the game. You can almost walk away and forget about them for 75 percent of the cook time.

 Preheat Oven 375°F

Serves 4

- 8 organic boneless skin-on chicken thighs, fat trimmed
- 2 teaspoons pink Himalayan salt
- Freshly cracked black pepper
- ½ teaspoon ground cumin
- 1 tablespoon avocado oil
- 3 sprigs fresh thyme
- 3 cloves garlic, peeled
- 2 tablespoons dry white wine
- 1 cup chicken broth or bone broth
- Peruvian Green Sauce (p. 134)

Season the chicken thighs on both sides with the salt and pepper. Season the flesh side only with the cumin.

Heat a large cast-iron skillet over medium heat. Add the avocado oil. Place the chicken thighs in the pan, skin side down, pressing gently against the flesh to ensure they get an even sear. Turn the heat down to medium-low.

No matter how tempted you are, do not move the chicken thighs at all for the next 20 minutes or so, until the skin has turned golden and crispy and the chicken thighs are almost cooked through.

At this point, flip each thigh over only once. Add the thyme sprigs and whole garlic gloves to the pan in between the chicken pieces. The thyme will pop and the garlic will sizzle. Cook for 2 minutes.

Preheat the oven to 375°F.

Carefully, so as not to pour any liquid on that hard-earned crispy skin, deglaze the pan with the white wine, followed by the chicken broth, by pouring it into the very edge of the skillet.

Cook the chicken thighs on the flesh side for 5 minutes more.

Transfer to the preheated oven and cook for 10 minutes more, until the juice has all but evaporated and cooked itself into the thighs, and the skin has deepened in color.

Remove the skillet from the oven and allow the thighs to rest in the pan for at least 5 minutes before serving.

Serve with a spoonful of the Peruvian Green Sauce smeared on the plate with the thighs on top so as to not disturb that golden crispy skin.

PERFECT CHICKEN BREAST

Truth be told, I'm not the biggest fan of chicken breasts, but when handled properly, chicken breasts have a unique flavor compared to thigh and the legs. That flavor doesn't usually shine through because we eat dry, overcooked chicken breasts. In my experience, the breasts need to be treated more like a dry, aged, bone-in steak than chicken, which is why we season and air dry overnight to allow for a great seal on the outside and, of course, crispy skin. The combination of the creamy pan sauce with the spicy, crunchy Macha Salsa creates a great balance.

 Preheat Oven 375°F

Serves 4

- 4 (10-ounce) skin-on bone-in chicken breasts
- 1 tablespoon sea salt, plus more for seasoning
- 1 teaspoon freshly cracked black pepper, plus more for seasoning
- ½ teaspoon granulated garlic
- ¼ teaspoon ground allspice
- 1 tablespoon avocado oil
- 3 or 4 sprigs fresh thyme

Pan Sauce:

- ½ teaspoon arrowroot starch
- 1 tablespoon cassava flour
- ½ cup canned coconut milk
- ½ cup chicken broth
- Juice of 1 lime

Cashew and Chile de árbol Salsa Macha (p. 132)

Sprinkle the chicken breasts all over with salt and place them on a rack over a dish in the refrigerator overnight. Do not cover; allow to air dry.

An hour before you are ready to cook the next day, remove the chicken breasts and sprinkle all over with the cracked pepper, granulated garlic, and allspice. Allow to come to room temperature, about 30 minutes.

Preheat the oven to 375°F.

In an ovenproof heavy-bottom skillet, preferably cast iron, heat the avocado oil over medium-high heat until just starting to smoke. Turn the heat down to medium. Add the chicken breasts to the pan, skin side down, and cook until golden brown, about 5 or 6 minutes.

Turn the breasts over and add the thyme sprigs. Immediately place the breasts in the oven and bake for about 10 to 12 minutes or until a thermometer stuck in the thickest part reads 145°F. Remove the chicken from the oven and allow to sit in the pan for 2 minutes, on the stove top.

Transfer the chicken breasts, still skin side up, to a cutting board and tent with foil. Allow to rest for 5 minutes more, enough time to prepare the pan sauce.

Make the pan sauce: There should be a good amount of natural chicken fat in the skillet. Remove enough to leave about 2 tablespoons in the skillet. Discard the thyme sprigs. Place the skillet over medium heat. Stir in the arrowroot starch and cassava flour and cook, stirring constantly, until the flours begin to turn golden brown, about 2 to 3 minutes. Slowly whisk in the coconut milk and chicken broth and bring to a simmer. Cook for 2 to 3 more minutes until thickened, continuing to stir. Add the lime juice and season with more salt and pepper. Set aside.

Carefully carve the breasts off the bones, being sure not to remove the skin. Slice each breast on a bias into ½-inch-thick slices.

Serve on top of a generous spoon of pan sauce. Drizzle with dots of Cashew and Chile de árbol Salsa Macha. I like eating this dish with my Almost Burned Butter Celeriac Root Purée (recipe follows).

ALMOST BURNED BUTTER CELERIAC ROOT PURÉE

Using brown butter in cooking adds such an amazing nutty and sweet flavor to whatever application, but what I love most is that essentially all the dairy and milk fat has been cooked out, leaving you with ghee. For this purée, I take it just a touch further to the point of almost burning the brown butter, leaving me with these little deep brown, almost black bits. I strain most of them out but add back just a few to give a nice char flavor and some pretty speckles too.

Serves 4

- 8 ounces grass-fed butter
- 2 medium celeriac roots, peeled and cubed to 1-inch
- 1 teaspoon sea salt
- 1 tablespoon coconut sugar
- 1 pinch ground cloves
- ½ cup coconut cream, plus additional if needed
- ¼ cup strained almost burned butter ghee plus ¼ teaspoon bits

Place the butter in a small saucepan and heat over medium-high heat. Stirring frequently, cook the butter until it turns a deep brown and the little bits of milk fat have all but cooked out, leaving an ash of milk fat in the bottom of the pan. The butter should still be translucent but deep brown and smell nutty and fragrant. Remove it from the heat the second it starts to smoke and immediately strain through a fine-mesh strainer into a shatterproof heat-resistant container. Be very careful when pouring; the butter is very hot! Allow it to cool slightly while you cook the celeriac root. Reserve a small pinch of the brown butter bits that were strained out and discard the rest.

Place the peeled cubed celeriac root in a medium pot and fill with just enough water to cover, without the cubes floating. Add the sea salt, coconut sugar, and cloves. Bring to a boil and reduce to a simmer. Cook the roots until all of the water has evaporated and the seasonings have cooked their way into the vegetables. Remove the pan from heat. The roots will be very overcooked. Transfer the mushy roots to a blender. Add the coconut cream, ¼ cup of the almost burned butter, and the pinch of little burned bits. Blend on high, scraping down frequently, until smooth and uniform. Add a bit more coconut cream or water if the mixture is too thick.

CHICKEN PICADILLO

Picadillo is one of my favorite things. The original is made with ground beef, potatoes, lots of added sugar, tomato paste, and a bunch of Sazón (Latin seasoning blend) and other seasonings. This version is a much lighter option made with ground organic chicken, fresh tomatoes, yucca, fresh herbs, and a few Mexican sun-dried spices—no processed seasonings. The secret swap-out here is the blanco tequila instead of red wine. Try topping with a few slices of hard-boiled eggs (see Cooking Eggs, p. 34).

 Preheat Oven 375°F

Serves 4

- 1 small pumpkin (about 2 ½ pounds), peeled, seeded, and diced into 1-inch cubes
- 5 tablespoons coconut oil, divided
- 1 ½ pounds organic ground chicken
- 1 tablespoon coconut sugar
- 1 teaspoon sea salt
- ½ teaspoon freshly cracked black pepper
- 1 medium yellow onion, peeled and diced into ¼-inch cubes
- 4 cloves garlic, minced
- 1 tablespoon ground cumin
- 1 teaspoon ground allspice
- 1 poblano chile pepper, seeded and diced into ¼-inch cubes
- ¾ cup blanco tequila (plus 1 shot for the cook)
- 1 cup diced plum tomatoes, cut into ¼-inch cubes
- ½ cup pimento-stuffed Spanish green olives, sliced
- ¼ cup capers, drained
- Additional sea salt and freshly cracked black pepper to taste

Preheat the oven to 375°F.

Toss the cubed pumpkin with 2 tablespoons of coconut oil.

Spread the pumpkin on a greased nonstick baking sheet and place in the preheated oven. Roast until just fork tender, about 15-20 minutes.

Remove from oven and allow to cool slightly.

In a large sauté pan, brown the ground chicken with 1 tablespoon of the coconut oil. Add the coconut sugar, sea salt, and cracked black pepper. Once cooked, using a slotted spoon, remove the ground chicken from the pan to a plate lined with paper towels.

Return the pan to heat and add the remaining 2 tablespoons oil. Add the onion and cook until soft, about 3 to 4 minutes. Add the garlic and cook until almost turning golden brown.

Add the ground cumin, ground allspice, and poblano pepper. Cook for 2 to 3 more minutes before folding in the roasted pumpkin pieces.

Add the cooked ground chicken back into the pan.

Deglaze the pan by adding the tequila. Be careful—it may flame up momentarily from the alcohol content! Once the tequila has reduced and the raw alcohol has cooked out, about 5 minutes, add the tomatoes, olives, and capers.

Continue to cook over medium heat, stirring occasionally until the sauce thickens, about 5-7 minutes more. Taste and adjust seasoning if needed.

CILANTRO CAULIFLOWER COCONUT RICE

Serves 2

- 1 medium head of cauliflower
- 1 tablespoon coconut oil
- ¼ cup carton coconut milk beverage
- Juice and zest of 1 lime
- 1 bunch fresh cilantro leaves finely chopped
- Salt and pepper to taste

Peel back the tough leaves from the cauliflower and cut the head into florets. Add the florets to a food processor and pulse until the cauliflower reaches the size and consistency of rice.

Heat the coconut oil in a large sauté pan over medium heat. Add the riced cauliflower and cook for 5 minutes until cauliflower is slightly tender. Make sure to stir frequently so the "rice" doesn't brown.

Add the coconut milk, lime juice, and zest. Reduce heat to low and allow to cook until most of the liquid has evaporated and the cauliflower rice is tender but not mushy.

Fold in the chopped fresh cilantro and season with salt and pepper to taste.

EASY CHICKEN TINGA (TACOS WITH JICAMA SHELLS)

Chicken Tinga is essentially shredded chicken in a sauce with a tomato and chile base. This classic Mexican dish is most often served piled high on top of crispy tortillas. Here is a taco-style application that I probably make once a week. Let me be clear that there is no proper substitution for real hand-pressed corn tortillas, and I believe strongly that when going out to eat Mexican cuisine, one should indulge in eating proper tacos made with corn tortillas. But if I want to cook tacos once a week, I have to be smart about it. I love this low-carb jicama "shell." The flavor and crunch of the jicama adds another layer to the dish that I really enjoy. You can also serve these with store-bought "carb smart" tortillas.

Preheat Oven 350°F

Serves 4

Chicken Tinga:

- 2 ½ pounds organic skinless bone-in chicken thighs
- 2 teaspoons sea salt, plus more for seasoning
- 1 teaspoon freshly cracked black pepper, plus more for seasoning
- 4 tablespoons avocado oil, divided
- 2 medium yellow onions, peeled and thinly sliced
- 4 cloves garlic, minced
- ½ teaspoon ground cumin
- ½ teaspoon chile de árbol powder
- ½ teaspoon dried Mexican oregano
- 1 ½ pounds Roma tomatoes, diced into ¼-inch cubes
- 2 chipotle chiles in adobo sauce, chopped, plus 1 tablespoon adobo sauce
- 2 cups chicken broth or bone broth
- Salt and pepper to taste

The Tacos:

- 1 large jicama root, peeled and thinly sliced
- 1 avocado, peeled, seeded, and thinly sliced
- ¼ cup Charred Green Onion Cashew Crema (see p. 37)
- ¼ pound crumbled cotija cheese (optional)

Garnishes:

- Chopped fresh cilantro
- Fresh lime wedges

Prepare the Tinga: Preheat the oven to 350°F.

Trim any excess fat from the chicken thighs and season all over with salt and pepper.

In a large heavy-bottom cast iron skillet or nonstick sauté pan, heat half the oil and add the chicken thighs, smooth side down. Cook and brown the thighs over medium-high heat for about 6 minutes. Flip the chicken thighs over and continue to cook for another 6 minutes.

Remove the chicken thighs from the pan and transfer to a 9 x 13 baking dish. Set aside.

Return the skillet to the heat and add the second half of the oil. Add the onions and cook over medium heat, stirring frequently, until they have softened, about 5 minutes. Add the garlic and cook for 1 minute more. Add the spices, tomatoes, chiles, adobo sauce, and chicken broth. Bring to a boil and reduce to a simmer. Cook for 30 minutes until the sauce has thickened slightly.

Remove the sauce from heat and allow to cool slightly for 10 to 15 minutes. Transfer half of the sauce to a food processor and blend until smooth and uniform. Season with salt and pepper. Return the blending sauce back to the pan with the unblended sauce and stir to combine.

Pour the sauce over the chicken thighs in the baking dish. Bake the chicken uncovered in the oven until the meat is tender and falling off the bone, and the sauce has thickened and darkened, about 1 hour.

Remove the dish from the oven and carefully transfer the chicken thighs to a cutting board. Using a pulling motion with a set of tongs (not a knife), gently shred the chicken; it should come right off the bone. Discard the bones. Return the pulled chicken to the sauce and stir to combine.

Prepare the tacos: Peel the jicama and, using a mandolin, cut into ⅛-inch-thick slices. Place in a bowl of cool water until ready to build the tacos. If using tortillas, wrap them in foil and warm them in the oven for 10 minutes.

Spoon about 2 to 3 tablespoons chicken onto each jicama round. Spoon a little of the sauce over the chicken. Place one slice of avocado on each taco. Drizzle with the Charred Green Onion Cashew Crema and then sprinkle with cotija cheese. Garnish with cilantro and serve with fresh lime wedges.

SLOW-COOKED PORK

This dish is also known as pernil, or lechon, or cochinita pibil, depending on where you are, and sometimes uses a whole baby pig instead of pork shoulder. Slow cooking any cut of pork isn't complicated, but it does require investing time. If you can manage to wait long enough, it will be worth it. The quality of the product is important too. What the animal eats and how it is raised affects the end flavor. Pork is relatively inexpensive, so look for higher-end products when ordering pork butt, belly, ribs, or chops.

Preheat Oven 400°F

Serves 6 to 8

Pibil Marinade:

- 12 cloves garlic, peeled, divided
- 1 cinnamon stick
- 2 teaspoons whole cumin seeds
- 4 whole cloves
- 2 ancho chile peppers, seeded
- 2 tablespoons dried oregano
- 6 tablespoons achiote paste
- 3 tablespoons apple cider vinegar
- ½ cup sour orange juice (from Seville oranges) or ¼ cup regular orange juice and ¼ cup freshly squeezed lime juice
- 1 tablespoon sea salt
- 1 tablespoon freshly cracked black pepper

Pork:

- 1 (3-pound) piece boneless pork shoulder or boneless leg, cut into 6 chunks
- Additional sea salt
- 3 or 4 banana leaves

Make the pibil marinade: Put 6 garlic cloves in a medium sauté pan with the cinnamon stick, cumin seeds, cloves, ancho chiles, and oregano. Dry roast the spices over medium heat, stirring constantly so they don't burn, for about 5 minutes. Transfer the roasted mixture to a blender along with the remaining 6 garlic cloves and achiote paste, and blend on high into a thick uniform paste.

Transfer to a bowl and stir in the vinegar and citrus juice. Add the salt and pepper.

Prepare the pork: Place the pork pieces in a dish that will fit in your refrigerator. Rub the pork all over with the marinade, tossing to make sure it is thoroughly coated. Cover with plastic wrap and refrigerate overnight, or for at least 4 hours.

Preheat the oven to 400°F.

Place a roasting pan full of water on the bottom shelf of the oven.

Line another roasting pan with the banana leaves, draping them over the edges. Transfer the marinated pork to the lined roasting pan. Fold the draped leaf ends over each other, covering the pork completely. Place another leaf on top if need be. Cover the roasting pan with a lid or foil and place in the oven on the middle shelf.

Roast the pork for 3 or 4 hours until the meat is tender and cooked through. Remove the pan from the oven and allow to cool almost completely on the stovetop without uncovering. The meat will continue to get more and more tender and the cooking juices will settle.

When the meat is cool, remove it from the pan and gently shred. Remove the banana leaf from the pan and reserve about 1 ½ cups of cooking juices. In a fresh pan, place the reserved cooking juices along with the shredded pork. Taste and season the pork if needed.

If serving now, heat up the pork in the pan on the stove top. If not, cover and refrigerate at this point.

I like to eat my slow-roasted pork in lettuce wraps with Pickled Onions and Peppers (p. 46) or Pickled Cucumbers and Green Papaya (p. 134). Try throwing some fresh mint and cilantro leaves inside the lettuce cup.

ALL-DAY COSTILLAS (RIBS)

I know it may feel like a huge commitment to cook something for 6 hours before you cook it again, but trust me, it is well worth it. These ribs only take 5 to 10 minutes to prep before you can throw them in the oven and go about your day. The result is the most delicious melt-in-your-mouth, meat-falling-off-the-bone ribs ever! The best part is when you are ready to eat, the fire time is only 15 minutes! I like doing the second cook in a large cast-iron pan over an open flame or grill, but doing it on the stovetop works just fine. You can also throw these in the oven right before bed, if you are an early riser. Don't bake them longer than 7 hours or the meat will be too tender and disintegrate when handling.

Preheat Oven 300°F

Serves 4

- 2 medium yellow onions, peeled and chopped
- 2 medium celery roots, peeled and chopped
- 1 medium carrot, peeled and chopped
- 1 medium ripe papaya, peeled, seeded, and chopped
- 10 cloves garlic, peeled and smashed
- 4 whole allspice berries
- 2 star anise pods
- 6 sprigs thyme
- 2 full racks natural baby back pork ribs (about 4 pounds)
- About 2 tablespoons sea salt
- Freshly cracked black pepper
- 12 ounces Jamaican or Mexican beer (1 bottle)
- 1 cup dark Jamaican rum
- ½ cup agave nectar
- 1 quart chicken broth or bone broth, plus water as needed
- Avocado oil
- Crispy Onion, Garlic, and Chile Oil (p. 65)
- 1 cup chopped fresh cilantro

Preheat the oven to 300°F.

Place the onions, celery roots, carrot, papaya, garlic, allspice, star anise, and thyme sprigs in the bottom of a roasting pan. Generously salt the ribs all over with sea salt and pepper, and lay the ribs side by side on top of the ingredients in the roasting pan. Pour the beer, rum, agave nectar, and chicken broth all over the ribs. Add enough water to just cover the ribs.

Cut a piece of parchment paper to nestle inside the roasting pan, covering the ribs. Cover the pan with foil and place the ribs in the oven.

Cook the ribs for 6 to 7 hours, until the ribs are tender and easily pierced with a knife.

Remove the foil and paper and put the ribs back in the oven. Increase the heat to 375°F and brown the ribs for 15 to 20 minutes.

Transfer the ribs from the pan to a cutting board to cool.

Strain the braising liquid, and transfer the strained liquid to a medium saucepan over medium heat. Skim off the fat as best you can. Cook until the liquid is reduced by half.

Once the ribs are cool, cut them into 2 or 3 rib pieces.

Place a cast iron skillet directly on your grill over an open flame, or on your stovetop over medium-high heat. Drizzle a small amount of avocado oil into the hot pan. Add the rib sections meat side down and sear for 3 to 4 minutes until a crust forms. (You will most likely have to do this in two batches, as all the ribs won't fit into the skillet at once.) Carefully flip the ribs over and ladle some of the braising liquid into the pan. Continue to cook and baste the ribs for another 10 minutes. The sauce will thicken and turn into a sticky glaze. If grilling, close the lid between bastings to allow the grill to impart some smoke flavor into the ribs.

Serve the sticky ribs with Crispy Onion, Garlic, and Chile Oil and top with chopped cilantro.

BRAISED OXTAILS, CUBAN STYLE

There seems to be a culinary application for oxtails in almost every single culture around the world. In India it's known as *dumghazah*; in Iran, *baghla-poli-machicheh*; in the Philippines, *kare kare*; in Cuba, *rabo encendido*; and in Korea, *kkori-gomtang*. The dish is popular in South Africa and in the southern United States. No matter where you are in the world, the dish is almost always a delicious slow-cooked stew served over some type of starch. Funny side story: Oxtails are my husband's favorite, and he grades each batch that I make. I think my best rating has only been two or three gold stars. Naturally my goal is to beat that. I like to serve these oxtails with Pumpkin Fufu (recipe follows).

Serves 4

- 5 pounds oxtails, disjointed to 2- or 3-inch pieces
- 1 cup dry white wine
- 2 tablespoons coconut oil
- 2 teaspoons sea salt
- 1 teaspoon ground cumin
- Freshly cracked black pepper
- 2 teaspoons avocado oil
- 2 medium yellow onions, peeled and diced
- 2 cups diced green bell peppers
- 2 cups diced red bell peppers
- 5 cloves garlic, minced
- 2 medium celery root, peeled and diced to 1-inch cubes
- 1 Scotch bonnet chile pepper, seeded and minced
- 1 teaspoon natural achiote paste (recado rojo)—no MSG!
- ¼ teaspoon ground cinnamon
- ½ teaspoon ground allspice
- ½ teaspoon ground nutmeg
- 1 dried avocado leaf or bay leaf
- 1 pound plum tomatoes, diced
- 1 quart beef broth or bone broth
- Additional sea salt and freshly cracked black pepper as needed

In a shallow dish, toss the oxtails with the white wine, coconut oil, salt, cumin, and black pepper. Cover and marinate in the refrigerator or for at least 4 hours or overnight.

Remove the oxtails from the marinade and discard the juices.

Heat a large pot over medium-high heat. Add a small amount of avocado oil, just enough to glisten the pan slightly. Brown the oxtails on both sides, in batches, for about 3 to 4 minutes per side. Set the seared oxtails aside.

In the same pot, add the onions and sauté over medium heat until soft and translucent. Add the bell peppers and garlic and sauté for a few minutes more, until the garlic is fragrant.

Add all the remaining ingredients to the pot, along with the browned oxtails, and enough water to ensure the oxtails are covered.

Bring to a boil and reduce to a simmer. Cover and braise for 2 to 3 hours until the oxtails are tender and beginning to pull away from the bone. Remove the avocado leaf before serving the oxtails. If the sauce is too soupy, take the oxtails out and set aside, and reduce the sauce by itself until thickened.

Serve the oxtails over a bed of Pumpkin Fufu (p. 127) with a thickened chunky sauce over them.

PUMPKIN FUFU

Serves 4

- 1 small pie pumpkin (about 2 ½ pounds), peeled, seeded, and diced into 1-inch cubes
- ¼ pound natural nitrate-free uncured bacon, diced
- 1 medium yellow onion, peeled and diced
- 4 cloves garlic, minced
- Sea salt and freshly cracked black pepper to taste

Place the pumpkin pieces in a medium pot and fill with enough salted water to cover. Bring to a boil and cook until the pumpkin is fork tender, about 12 to 14 minutes. Drain the pumpkin into a colander and discard the cooking water. Transfer the pumpkin to a bowl and mash using a root masher or the back of a spoon. Set aside.

Heat a medium sauté pan over medium heat and add the bacon pieces. Cook the bacon until it has turned brown but is not fully crispy, and most of the fat has rendered out. Drain off most of the rendered fat, just leaving about 1 tablespoon in the pan, being careful not to lose any of the bacon bits.

Add the diced onion and garlic, and sauté for 5 minutes or so until the onion is soft and translucent.

Remove the pan from heat and add the mashed pumpkin to the pan. Gently fold the mixture until uniform and smooth. Adjust seasoning if needed. Transfer the mixture to a serving dish and keep warm, covered on the stove until ready to serve.

CHURRASCO with CHIMICHURRI

Although you will find a version of churrasco in a lot of Latin cultures, it actually originated in Brazil. The term is Portuguese for "grilled meat." Churrasco is typically made with flank or skirt steak, but I also enjoy making this with a nice rib cap or hanger steak. All of these cuts do well with the marinating process. The end result of a marinated churrasco-style steak is quite different on the palate and goes well with the vibrant herbaceous Chimichurri Sauce. I also enjoy eating churrasco with some grilled radishes and green onions too. Serve it alongside the Coconut Creamed Greens (recipe follows).

Serves 4

- 10 cloves garlic, peeled
- 1 teaspoon sea salt
- ½ teaspoon black peppercorns
- ½ cup orange juice from sour oranges (Seville oranges) or ¼ cup regular orange juice and ¼ cup freshly squeezed lime juice
- ½ cup diced white onion
- 1 teaspoon ground cumin
- 1 teaspoon dried oregano
- ½ cup avocado oil
- 2 pounds grass-fed skirt steak, cut into 4 portions
- 1 recipe Chimichurri Sauce (p. 142)

Make the marinade: Using a mortar and pestle (or a blender if you don't have one), mash/pulse the garlic cloves, salt, and pepper into a paste. Add the citrus juice, onion, cumin, and oregano and stir just to combine. Transfer the mixture to a bowl and whisk in the avocado oil. Allow the mixture to sit for 15 minutes to allow the flavors to come together.

Make the churrasco: Place the skirt steak portions in a shallow dish and add enough of the marinade to cover the meat. Wrap the dish in plastic wrap and refrigerate for at least 4 hours or overnight.

When ready to cook the steak, remove it from the marinade and wipe off some of the excess oil, so that your grill doesn't flare up. Preheat the grill to high heat. Wait until the coals have turned white, this will ensure less flame up and the highest heat possible.

Grill the meat to your preferred temperature. I prefer medium rare, which will take about 4 minutes per side. I also like a little cross hatching, giving more good seared flavor on the meat. Try laying the meat down, cooking for 2 minutes, then turning the meat 45 degrees, and cooking 2 minutes more. Then flip, and do the same. Once you pull the steak off the grill, allow it to rest for at least 5 minutes before slicing. When ready to slice, cut the steak at a 45-degree angle, on a bias, against the grain.

You can also cook your churrasco on a cast-iron grill pan on your stove. Any time you cook a marinated meat on the stove, be prepared for some smoke, and set your fans to high!

Serve the steak with Chimichurri Sauce, my favorite sauce on the planet.

COCONUT CREAMED GREENS

I've opened my fair share of steakhouses in my career, and I probably could cook steak in my sleep at this point. But I still enjoy a date night out at a steakhouse, with the choice of different cuts of meat and a swarm of rich and indulgent sides. One of my favorites is creamed spinach. Decadent and heavy, it tastes amazing in the moment, but the guilt settles in quickly. I love this version because it hits the spot and I can feel good about eating it.

Serves 4

- 2 tablespoons coconut oil
- 1 medium yellow onion, peeled and diced into ¼-inch pieces
- 3 cloves garlic, minced
- ¼ teaspoon red pepper flakes
- 1 teaspoon chopped fresh thyme leaves
- ¼ teaspoon ground nutmeg
- Pinch of ground cloves
- ½ cup chicken broth or bone broth
- ¾ cup coconut cream
- 1 teaspoon arrowroot starch or 1 tablespoon cassava flour
- 1 pound cleaned and chopped greens, such as collard greens, kale, spinach, callaloo, or use a combo!
- Sea salt and freshly cracked black pepper to taste

In a medium saucepan, heat the coconut oil over medium heat. Add the onion, garlic, red pepper flakes, and thyme. Sauté until the onion becomes soft and translucent, about 5 minutes.

Add the nutmeg and cloves, and cook for 1 minutes more.

Add the chicken broth and coconut cream and bring to a simmer. Slowly whisk in the arrowroot starch. Allow the sauce to simmer for about 5 minutes, until it starts to thicken.

Fold in the chopped greens and allow the mixture to cook for another 10 to 12 minutes until the greens have wilted completely and the flavors have come together. The sauce should be thick and bubbly, not too runny.

Season with salt and pepper to taste.

MACKEREL VERA CRUZ STYLE

Like most coastal regions in the world, Vera Cruz's cuisine is heavily based on its fresh fish. And like most Latin American countries, the food has a large Old World influence. For example, *pescado a la Veracruzana*, a staple dish, displays Spanish and Italian influences with its plum tomatoes, olives, and capers. It's a delightful marriage of fresh fish, usually snapper, and a tangy stewed tomato sauce. The first time I used mackerel in this dish was during my final dinner service on my winning season of *Hell's Kitchen*. The intense nature of mackerel stands up really well to this briny, acidic sauce. This is why it is important to buy only super-fresh mackerel. I like serving this dish along with some buttery little gem lettuces, brushed lightly with a lemon olive oil and grilled briefly just before eating.

Serves 2

- 4 (6-ounce) mackerel fish fillets
- Flake sea salt
- 2 tablespoons coconut oil
- 1 medium white onion, diced into ¼-inch pieces
- 3 cloves garlic very thinly sliced, preferably using a mandolin
- 16 ounces fresh plum tomatoes, peeled, seeded, and diced into ¼-inch pieces
- 1 ½ ounces mezcal
- 1 bay leaf
- 1 teaspoon dried Mexican oregano
- 1 teaspoon coconut sugar
- ½ teaspoon ground cinnamon
- ¼ teaspoon ground cumin
- ½ cup Spanish green olives, pitted and sliced, plus 1 teaspoon brine
- 1 tablespoon capers plus brine
- Sea salt and freshly cracked black pepper to taste
- Avocado oil spray

Garnish:

- Fresh cilantro sprigs

Using a sharp paring knife, make 3 or 4 shallow slits through the mackerel skin on each filet, being careful not to cut too deep into the flesh. Pat the filets dry and sprinkle both sides with flake sea salt. Place the fish on a small rack over a plate (if you don't have a rack, just use the plate) and refrigerate for 30 minutes. This allows the salt to slightly cure the exterior of the fish ahead of cooking.

While the fish is curing, make the Vera Cruz Sauce: Heat a medium sauté pan over medium heat. Add the coconut oil and onion, and cook until the onion has softened and become translucent, about 5 minutes. Add the shaved garlic and cook for 1 minute more. Add the tomatoes and cook for 2 minutes.

Deglaze the pan with the shot of mezcal, (be careful—it may flame up). Cook out the raw alcohol for 1 to 2 minutes before adding the bay leaf, Mexican oregano, and coconut sugar, cinnamon, and cumin to the pan. Bring to a simmer and cook for 15 minutes until the sauce has thickened and most of the tomato liquid has cooked out. Add the olives, capers, and brine, and cook for 5 minutes more. Remove from heat and season with sea salt and pepper. Set aside.

Heat a cast-iron grill pan over medium-high heat. Once hot, spray lightly with avocado oil spray, just enough to grease the pan so that the fish doesn't stick.

Remove the excess flake salt and moisture from the fish filets. Place the fish into the hot greased grill pan skin side down, and sear for 2 minutes. Use the back of a spoon to gently lift the skin up from the pan, to ensure the skin is not stuck. Lift the filets and rotate 45°F, still cooking on the skin side for 2 more minutes. This will create some beautiful crisscross grill marks and evenly crisp the skin in places, while still leaving some sections of silvery blue skin visible.

In one motion, use your spoon to flip the fish filets over onto the flesh side. Cook for 2 to 3 minutes until the fish is just cooked through. I prefer mackerel cooked medium, with the tiniest bit of an undercooked center, similar to other oily fish like salmon or swordfish.

Remove the filets from the pan and stack two filets on each plate off to one side. Spoon the chunky Vera Cruz Sauce along the opposite edge of the plate all along one edge, in a crescent shape. Plating like this showcases the beautiful fish and sauce, allowing you to break off bites and drag them through as much sauce as you'd like, without smothering the fish. Traditionally, the fish is actually baked in the sauce, but I love how pretty the plate looks more deconstructed.

Garnish with fresh sprigs of cilantro.

SHRIMP AND "GRITS"

I was introduced to southern-style cooking by my dad Billy's family. Billy made grits for me about once a week, and they were so good—especially since they were filled with cream and butter and cheese! I still indulge in grits for breakfast occasionally if I find them on a brunch menu topped with an egg and a pork product—I can't help myself. This version of shrimp and grits eases the guilt by swapping out the heavy grits for some simply prepared Creamed Yucca (recipe follows). I also revised the dredging mix for the shrimp to exclude the gluten and flour, and I use nitrate-free uncured natural bacon instead of ham.

Serves 4

- ¼ cup coconut flour
- 1 tablespoon sea salt
- ¼ teaspoon Jerk Seasoning (p. 86)
- ½ teaspoon freshly cracked black pepper
- 1 tablespoon coconut oil
- ¼ pound nitrate-free, natural uncured smoked bacon, diced into ¼-inch pieces
- 1½ pounds large (26–30 count) shrimp, peeled and deveined
- 1 small shallot, peeled and minced
- 1 clove garlic, peeled and minced
- 6 to 8 shishito peppers, stems removed and sliced ¼ inch thick
- ¼ cup thinly sliced green onions (white and green parts)
- ½ cup to 1 cup chicken broth or bone broth, or vegetable or seafood broth
- ¼ teaspoon arrowroot starch or 1 tea spoon cassava flour
- Juice of 1 lemon
- Additional sea salt and freshly cracked black pepper to taste
- Creamed Yucca (p. 134)

Combine the coconut flour, sea salt, Jerk Seasoning, and black pepper in a mixing bowl and set aside.

In a large sauté pan, heat the coconut oil over medium heat. Add the bacon and cook, stirring occasionally, until the bacon has browned and the fat has rendered, about 5 minutes.

Dredge the cleaned shrimp in the dry mixture and shake off any extra. Quickly but carefully, add the shrimp to the pan and cook for 2 minutes on the first side.

Flip each shrimp over, again working quickly, using tongs or a kitchen spoon. Add the shallot, garlic, and shishito peppers, and cook until the second side of the shrimp is browned, about 2 to 3 more minutes, and the vegetables begin to soften.

Add the green onions and the chicken broth and bring up to a high simmer. Cook until the shrimp are cooked through and the sauce has reduced by about one third. Whisk in the arrowroot starch with a fork. Add the lemon juice and season with salt and pepper.

Divide the yucca among shallow bowls, and spoon the shrimp mixture over the yucca along with the sauce around the edge of the bowls.

CREAMED YUCCA

Serves 4

- 2 large yucca roots, peeled and sliced into 2-inch pieces
- 1 tablespoon Himalayan pink salt
- 3 whole green onions
- 2 tablespoons avocado oil
- Additional sea salt and freshly cracked black pepper to taste
- ¼ cup coconut cream

Fill a medium pot with enough water to cover the yucca and add pink salt. Set over medium-high heat and add the yucca. Bring to a boil and cook until fork tender, about 20 minutes.

Drain the yucca, discarding most of the starchy water, but reserving a few tablespoons. (The starchy water will be added later to make the mixture more creamy.)

While the yucca is cooking, place the whole green onions over an open-flame burner on the stove, or under a broiler, turning frequently, until charred and softened, about 5 minutes. Remove from heat and trim the root. Mince the green onions while they are still warm into a paste. Set aside.

Transfer the cooked yucca roots to a large bowl. Add the charred onion paste and avocado oil, and mash with the back of a wooden spoon. Season with some sea salt and some freshly cracked pepper if necessary, but the yucca should be well flavored from cooking in the salt water.

Add the coconut cream and stir until uniform. The mixture should be smooth and creamy, yet light and airy, with a few small chunky pieces.

ROASTED SPAGHETTI SQUASH

🔥 Preheat Oven 400°F

Serves 4

- 1 large (3-pound) spaghetti squash
- 1 tablespoon coconut oil
- 1 teaspoon fine sea salt

Preheat the oven to 400°F.

Cut the squash in half, lengthwise, and scoop out the seeds.

Rub the insides of each half with the coconut oil and sprinkle with sea salt.

Place the squash cut side down on a parchment lined baking sheet. Use a paring knife to slice three or four holes in the back side of each squash half.

Roast until fork tender and lightly browned on the outside, approximately 45 minutes.

Remove the squash from the oven and flip them over. Allow the squash to cool slightly. When cool enough to hold, scrape all of the noodle-like flesh out of the shells. Fluff apart the squash strands.

WHOLE GRILLED FISH

Johnny Cay is one of my most beloved cays in the San Andrés Bay. It's surrounded by a well-preserved and dense ecosystem providing incredible feasts of urchin, conch, and, of course, a variety of flaky white fish perfect for grilling. I will never forget my first memories of eating a whole fish grilled over a firepit on Johnny Cay—fingers burning as I pulled off a scored cube of fish while sitting on the whitest sand beach I have ever seen.

There are only a few steps to grilling a beautiful whole fish. Simply follow these guidelines and you will have a showstopping result that you can serve with just about any fresh salsa. Most importantly, make sure your grill is clean and seasoned well with a kitchen towel dipped in avocado oil. You don't want to dirty the fish with old char flavor, and the skin is less likely to stick on a clean grill.

Serves 4

- 1 (about 4-pound) red snapper or rock fish, gutted, cleaned, and scaled
- Plenty of coconut oil or avocado oil
- Flake sea salt

Preheat the grill to high heat.

Score the flesh of the fish by using a sharp knife to cut slits on a bias from fins to belly, vertically across the fish every 2 inches along the whole length of the body. Flip the fish over and repeat on the other side.

Rub the fish all over very generously with coconut oil, making sure to rub inside the slits as well. The entire surface of the fish should be coated so that it doesn't stick to the grill. Sprinkle the fish on both sides with flake sea salt.

When the grill is hot, but still not flaming too much, place the fish on the grill with the body stretching across the grates. Once you put it down don't touch it! The grill will slowly cook the fish while crisping up the skin at the same time. Don't rush it.

Once the first side appears to be crispy and blistered (you will be able to see it at the edges), use a spatula to gently lift the edge of the fish slightly off the grill. If it lifts off the grill easily, that means it is ready to flip. If it is still stuck, it's not ready. This first side can take anywhere from 12 to 15 minutes for a larger fish.

Once you have done the lift check, use the long spatula to loosen the fish all along the edge and then flip in one motion up and away from your body. Once you have flipped the fish, don't move it again until the second side is also ready, another 12 minutes or so.

When the fish is cooked, carefully slide the long grill spatula under the fish lengthwise and lift it onto a platter immediately.

Finish with another sprinkle of flake salt and serve with any fresh salsa, such as the Avocado-Papaya Salsa on p. 140.

CURRIED GREEN PLANTAINS AND JACKFRUIT

I grew up eating curry at least once a week. My mom used a delicious compressed curry spice block folded into chicken broth along with chicken and vegetables. We ate it with a drizzle of tangy yogurt, spicy peanuts, sweet raisins, and cubed avocado. Sometimes the curry would accompany a mango or apricot chutney. And of course, we piled it on mounds of white rice. The meal was delightful but a little heavy on the carbs. I make my own curry now and serve it over a bed of roasted spaghetti squash. I like to add a drizzle of plain vegan yogurt over the top to cut the spice.

Serves 4

- 1 tablespoon coconut oil
- 1 small white onion, peeled and diced into ½-inch pieces
- 2 cloves garlic, peeled and shaved thin
- 1 teaspoon coconut sugar
- ½ cup chopped fresh cilantro leaves
- 1 teaspoon organic curry powder
- 1 teaspoon turmeric
- ¼ teaspoon ground cumin
- 1 teaspoon garam masala
- ½ teaspoon ground allspice
- 2 green plantains, peeled and sliced
- 2 (20-ounce) cans prepared green jack-fruit, drained and pulled
- 1 Scotch bonnet or habanero chile pep-per, seeded and minced
- 1 cup coconut water
- ½ cup canned coconut milk
- Sea salt and freshly cracked black pep-per to taste
- 2 tablespoons freshly squeezed lime juice

Garnishes:

- Cashew yogurt (optional)
- Chopped fresh mint leaves
- Toasted sliced almonds

Heat the coconut oil in a large wide sauté pan over medium heat. Add the onion and garlic, and cook for 1 to 2 minutes, until onion is beginning to soften and garlic is fragrant. Stir in the coconut sugar, cilantro, and spices. Cook until the sugar has dissolved and the spices form a paste in the pan, about 3 minutes.

Add the plantain and pulled jackfruit. Stir until the plantains and jackfruit are well coated in the paste and beginning to caramelize slightly on the outside, about 2 to 3 minutes.

Add the Scotch bonnet chile pepper and coconut water and bring up to a boil, then reduce to a simmer and cover. Cook for 10 minutes.

Add the coconut milk, and at this point season to taste with sea salt and freshly cracked black pepper. Return lid and cook for 10 minutes more, or until plantains have softened and the sauce has thickened.

Stir in the lime juice. Garnish with a drizzle of cashew yogurt, mint leaves, and toasted sliced almonds. Serve on a bed of roasted spaghetti squash (recipe follows).

AVOCADO–PAPAYA SALSA

Serve this salsa chilled with fresh grilled whole fish or any other grilled or broiled seafood. It can also be eaten as a side dish or salad.

Makes 6 cups

- 1 small ripe papaya, peeled, seeded, and diced into ½-inch pieces
- 2 avocados, ripe but firm, peeled, pitted, and diced into ½-inch pieces
- 1 Scotch bonnet chile pepper, stemmed, seeded, and minced
- ½ cup chopped fresh cilantro leaves
- ¼ cup finely diced red onion (¼-inch pieces)
- ¼ cup freshly squeezed lime juice
- ½ ounce Cointreau (or other orange liqueur)
- ⅛ cup extra-virgin olive oil or avocado oil
- Sea salt to taste

Combine all ingredients in a medium non-reactive bowl. Season with salt to taste. This salsa is best served fresh, but can be made up to 4 hours ahead.

CASHEW AND CHILE DE ÁRBOL SALSA MACHA

Makes 1 cup

- 3 tablespoons coconut oil
- ¼ cup roasted unsalted cashews
- 6 dried árbol chile peppers, stemmed
- 1 ancho chile pepper, stemmed
- ¼ teaspoon dried Mexican oregano
- 3 whole allspice berries
- 6 cloves garlic, peeled
- 1 medium white onion, peeled and diced
- 1 teaspoon freshly squeezed lime juice
- 1 tablespoon freshly squeezed orange juice
- 1 teaspoon sea salt

Heat the coconut oil in a medium sauté pan over medium heat. Add the cashews, chile peppers, herbs and spices, garlic, and onion. Cook, stirring frequently, until the onion is soft, about 5 or 6 minutes. Transfer the mixture to a blender. Add the citrus juices and salt and pulse on medium until uniform but still a tiny bit chunky, about 2 minutes. This salsa will keep for up to 1 week in the refrigerator, in an airtight container. Bring the salsa to room temperature before using, as needed, and stir as it will have separated.

CHIMICHURRI SAUCE

This is probably my favorite sauce on the planet. Chimichurri Sauce is so versatile and goes well with any type of grilled protein. There is no single type of herb that you have to use, so feel free to mix it up to your liking, but the version below is close to the original one from Argentina. This sauce is very tangy on its own; it's meant to be paired with grilled meats and fish, so it stands up nicely against the hearty flavors of the proteins.

Makes 1 quart

- ¼ cup red wine vinegar
- Juice and zest of 1 lime
- 1 bunch fresh cilantro, leaves only (about 2 cups), divided
- 1 bunch fresh flat-leaf parsley, leaves only (about 2 cups), divided
- 4 large cloves garlic
- 1 teaspoon sea salt
- ½ teaspoon freshly cracked black pepper
- 1 teaspoon red pepper flakes
- ½ bunch fresh oregano, leaves only (about ½ cup)
- ½ bunch fresh mint, leaves only (about ½ cup)
- 1 cup extra-virgin olive oil or avocado oil

In a food processor, add the vinegar, lime juice, lime zest, half of the cilantro and parsley, along with the garlic, salt, black pepper, and red pepper flakes. Process until smooth and uniform.

Add the remaining cilantro and parsley, as well as the oregano, mint, and olive oil. Pulse until all the herbs are coarsely chopped, but not gritty on the tongue. The sauce should be uniform in texture, but slightly chunky.

CRISPY ONION, GARLIC, AND CHILE OIL

Makes 1 cup

- 2 árbol chile peppers, stemmed and seeded
- ½ cup avocado oil
- 4 cloves garlic, minced
- 1 cup dried gluten-free crispy onions
- 2 teaspoons crushed red pepper flakes
- ½ teaspoon paprika
- Sea salt and freshly cracked black pepper

In a small sauté pan, dry toast the árbol chiles over medium heat for 3 to 4 minutes. The skin will begin to turn light brown and blister. Remove from heat and place in a molcajete (mortar and pestle) or a food processor.

In the same pan, heat the avocado oil over medium heat, and add the minced garlic. Stirring vigorously, but carefully, allow the garlic to cook until it turns golden brown. Immediately remove from heat and transfer the garlic to the molcajete or the food processor with the chiles. Add the crispy onions, red pepper flakes, and paprika, and grind or pulse into a chunky paste. Season with sea salt and pepper to taste.

PERUVIAN GREEN SAUCE (AJI VERDE)

There's a magical moment when someone tries this sauce at a restaurant for the first time. It's tangy, a little spicy, herby, and creamy—it will surely become one of your go-to sauces, and you'll find yourself dipping just about anything in it. My favorite pairings are chicken and my Crispy Oven-Baked Patacones (p. 80). You can make it with Cashew Crema (p. 37), or you can use mayonnaise made with olive oil if you prefer.

Makes 1 ½ cups

- ¼ cup Plain Cashew Crema (p. 37) or real mayonnaise made with olive oil
- 2 cups cilantro leaves, no stems (about 1 large bunch)
- 4 cloves garlic, peeled
- 1 serrano chile pepper, stemmed, seeds removed
- 1 tablespoon aji amarillo paste (found in ethnic markets)
- 1 teaspoon fine sea salt
- Juice of 2 limes
- Splash of apple cider vinegar
- ½ ripe avocado, peeled and roughly chopped
- 2 tablespoons avocado oil
- Sea salt and freshly cracked pepper, to taste

Combine all ingredients in a high-powered blender. Blend until the herbs are almost completely broken down, and the sauce is bright green and creamy. It will still have a bit of texture. Taste and adjust seasoning to your liking. Cover and refrigerate for up to 1 week.

PICKLED CUCUMBERS AND GREEN PAPAYA

This condiment is wonderfully versatile, and can be found on my table often. Pickled things are great for cutting spice and I like to use them cold to balance out heat and texture.

Makes 1 quart

- 1 medium young unripe papaya (green), peeled, seeded, quartered, and sliced thin
- 1 English cucumber, unpeeled, sliced thin
- 2 cups apple cider vinegar
- 1 tablespoon pink Himalayan salt
- 1 Thai chile pepper, halved
- 1 clove peeled garlic, smashed

Place the sliced papaya and cucumber in a mixing bowl. Add the vinegar, salt, chile, and garlic. Stir to mix well. Cover the mixture with plastic wrap and place in the refrigerator to marinate for at least 2 hours before using. This mix will last up to two weeks, refrigerated.

DESSERTS

Most Latin and Caribbean desserts are heavy and overloaded with sugar. These versions, using much healthier ingredients and substitutions, make a lighter, joyful finish to your meal. Note that not every substitution is necessary—if you want to use dairy grass-fed butter instead of vegan cashew butter, by all means, live your best life. Every recipe in this section is gluten-free as written but can be made with wheat flour too. My dad and husband both have a huge sweet tooth, and every one of these recipes satisfies their cravings.

- Rum Cake
- Blackberry and Cho Cho Pie with Crumble Topping
- Flaky Pie Crust
- Coconut Tres Leches Cake
- Coconut Cream Whipped Cream
- Plátanos Calados
- Lemon Cake
- Pumpkin "Carrot Cake"
- Cocoa-Avocado Mousse
- Island Tea–Infused No-Milk Flan
- Homemade Nut Butter Cookies

RUM CAKE

I tasted the original version of this rum-soaked delight at a Caribbean craft fair years ago. This cake also works as an upside-down cake if you want to add slices of tropical fruit to the bottom of the pan before pouring the batter in to bake. I recommend trying sliced dragon fruit or thinly sliced grapefruit instead of the usual pineapple. But honestly, I prefer this cake on its own lathered in rum syrup, which I make using homemade fruit molasses. Lastly, make sure to use a high-quality organic instant pudding mix in the batter. You can even find a few good keto versions (I like Simply Delish natural puddings).

Preheat Oven 325°F

Makes 1 10-inch rum Bundt cake, 8 servings

Cake:

- Coconut oil spray
- 3 cups coconut flour (or a fifty-fifty mix of coconut and cassava flour), plus enough to flour the pan
- 2 ½ teaspoons baking powder
- ½ teaspoon sea salt
- ½ cup organic vanilla instant pudding mix
- ⅓ cup coconut shortening
- ⅓ cup vegan cashew butter or dairy grass-fed butter
- 1 ¾ cups coconut sugar or ¾ cup monk fruit sugar
- 4 large organic eggs
- 1 ½ teaspoons vanilla extract
- ½ cup dark Jamaican rum
- ½ cup water
- ¼ cup coconut oil
- 1 cup chopped macadamia nuts (optional)

Glaze:

- ¼ pound vegan cashew butter or dairy grass-fed butter
- ¼ cup water
- ⅓ cup homemade Papaya Molasses (p. 52) or agave syrup
- ½ cup overproof rum (I like Smith & Cross Jamaican Rum – Navy Strength)

Make the cake: Preheat the oven to 325°F. Grease and flour a 10-inch Bundt pan with coconut oil spray and coconut flour.

Combine the coconut flour, baking powder, salt, and dry pudding mix in a large bowl and set aside.

In a stand mixer fitted with the paddle attachment or in a separate mixing bowl using a hand mixer, cream the shortening, butter and sugar on medium-high speed until pale in color and fluffy, about 5 minutes.

Add the eggs one at a time, with the speed on medium, scraping down the sides between additions. Add the vanilla.

In a small bowl or measuring cup, combine the rum, water, and coconut oil.

Running the mixer on low speed, beginning with the dry ingredients, alternate adding the dry mixture and the rum mixture to the butter mixture in three additions. Scrape down the sides of the bowl between each addition.

If using the chopped macadamia nuts, sprinkle them into the greased and floured pan. Pour the batter into the pan over the nuts. Bake for 1 hour, or until a knife or skewer inserted into the cake comes out clean.

Remove the cake from the oven and allow to cool in the pan slightly while making the glaze.

Make the glaze: Combine all the glaze ingredients in a small saucepan and bring to a simmer. Cook for 4 or 5 minutes, until syrupy and the raw alcohol flavor is cooked out. Remove from heat and allow to cool slightly. It should still be warm when it's poured on the cake.

Pop the cake out of the pan and onto a serving plate or cake platter. Using a knife or skewer, poke holes all over the top of the cake.

Reserve a small amount of glaze for later, about ¼ cup. Spoon about ¼ cup of the remaining hot glaze all over the cake. As the cake absorbs the glaze, continue to spoon more until all the glaze is used. Once the cake is cool and the remaining ¼ cup of glaze is almost to room temperature and lukewarm, spoon the final, now thickened, glaze over the top of the cake, letting it drip down the sides.

Once the glaze has set, cut and serve!

For an extra treat, serve with a scoop of rum raisin ice cream on top.

BLACKBERRY AND CHO CHO PIE WITH CRUMBLE TOPPING

Nothing brings me more nostalgia than biting into a piece of my grandmother's blackberry pie—or the apple crisps made by my other grandmother in the south. It seemed only fitting that I combine the two and find a way to cut out some of the guilt. The chayote eat just like an apple in this pie.

Preheat Oven 400°F

Makes 1 (9-inch) pie

Pie Filling:
- 2 medium chayote squash, peeled
- 2 cups water
- 1 ½ cup coconut sugar or ¾ cup monk fruit sugar
- 2 whole cloves
- 3 whole allspice berries
- 2 pints blackberries
- ½ teaspoon ground cinnamon
- ⅛ teaspoon ground cloves
- ¼ teaspoon ground nutmeg
- ⅛ teaspoon ground allspice
- 2 tablespoons freshly squeezed lime juice
- 2 tablespoons arrowroot starch
- ¼ teaspoon sea salt
- 2 tablespoons vegan cashew butter or dairy grass-fed butter, chopped
- 1 recipe Flaky Pie Crust (recipe follows), par-baked as directed

Crumble Topping:
- ½ cup coconut sugar or ¼ cup monk fruit sugar
- ¾ cup almond flour
- ½ cup cubed cold vegan cashew butter or dairy grass-fed butter
- 2 tablespoons gluten-free quick cooking oats

Make the pie filling: In a small pot over medium heat, place the whole peeled chayote squash, water, ½ cup of the coconut sugar, whole cloves, and allspice berries. Bring up to a boil and reduce to a simmer. Cook for 10 minutes. Remove the chayote from the cooking water and allow to cool before slicing into ¼-inch-thick slices.

Preheat the oven to 400°F.

In a large bowl, combine the squash, blackberries, and the remaining ½ cup coconut sugar. Add the ground spices, lime juice, arrowroot starch, salt, and chopped butter. Once combined, pile the filling into the par-baked pie crust.

Make the crumble topping: In a food processor or in a bowl by hand with your fingers, pulse and combine the crumble topping ingredients until a lumpy sand like texture is achieved. Sprinkle the topping all over the top of the pie filling.

Bake the pie until bubbly around the edges, and until the crumble topping is a deep golden brown, 30 to 40 minutes. Allow to cool to room temperature before cutting.

FLAKY PIE CRUST

This pie crust alternate can be used for a variety of sweet and savory pies, and it works well as the upper crust of fully enclosed pies.

 Preheat Oven 350°F

Makes 1 (9-inch) pie

- Coconut oil pan spray
- ¼ cup ice water as needed
- 2 ½ cups coconut flour (or fifty-fifty almond flour and coconut flour), plus additional for dusting the work surface
- 1 teaspoon sea salt
- ⅓ cup coconut sugar or ¼ cup monk fruit sugar
- 10 tablespoons cold European-style vegan butter or dairy grass-fed butter, cubed
- 1 large organic egg
- ½ teaspoon vanilla extract (for sweet pies)

Preheat the oven to 350°F. Grease a 9-inch pie pan with coconut oil spray.

Place all ingredients into a food processor, starting with half of the ice water. Pulse the ingredients until they come together into a ball. If the mixture does not come together, add the remaining ice water and pulse again.

Transfer the dough ball onto a coconut-floured surface. Press into a disk. Flip the disk to coat in coconut flour. Place the dough disk between two pieces of parchment paper and roll out to 12 inches in diameter, large enough to fill the bottom and sides of a 9-inch pie pan.

Place the dough sheet, still between pieces of parchment paper, into the refrigerator and chill for 45 minutes.

Carefully remove one sheet of the parchment paper. Press the chilled dough disk, paper side up, into the prepared pie pan, pressing up and just over the sides. Remove the second sheet of parchment paper.

Par-bake the crust for 10 to 12 minutes. Allow to cool before filling. The par-baked pie crust can be stored at this point in the refrigerator until ready to use, if baking within 24 hours, or in the freezer for up to 1 month. Make sure to thaw completely before filling.

COCONUT TRES LECHES CAKE

I have been playing around with this riff on a tres leches cake for a long time. Once I got my husband's and father-in-law's stamp of approval, I never looked back! To be honest, when I make this, I still use heavy dairy cream for the topping. In fact, this is the only recipe I make using cow's milk cream. However, I have included a coconut whipped cream recipe, which is also delicious on this cake.

 Preheat Oven 350°F

Serves 6 to 8

Cake:

- Coconut oil spray
- Coconut flour, for preparing the dish
- 2 tablespoons honey or homemade Papaya Molasses (p. 52)
- ¼ pound coconut shortening
- 4 tablespoons European-style vegan cashew butter or dairy grass-fed butter
- 1 ½ cups finely ground almond flour
- 1 ½ cups coconut flour
- 2 teaspoons baking powder
- 1 teaspoon sea salt
- 10 large organic eggs
- 1 ½ cups coconut sugar or ¾ cup monk fruit sugar
- 2 teaspoons vanilla extract

Milk Soak:

- 2 (13.5 ounce) cans coconut milk
- 2 cups cashew milk or almond milk
- 1 (14-ounce) can sweetened condensed coconut milk (such as Nature's Charm)

Whipped Topping:

- 2 cups grass-fed dairy heavy cream
- 2 tablespoons powdered monk fruit sugar
- 1 teaspoon vanilla extract

Garnishes:

- Fresh lime zest
- Toasted coconut

Preheat the oven to 350°F. Grease with coconut oil spray and dust with coconut flour a decorative 9-inch square ceramic baking dish.

Make the cake: In a medium microwave-safe bowl, add the honey, coconut shortening, and butter. Microwave on high for 30 seconds to 1 minute, until melted. Stir and set aside.

In a large bowl, combine the flours, baking powder, and sea salt. Set aside.

In a stand mixer fitted with the paddle attachment, or in a separate large bowl using a hand mixer with the beater attachments, beat the eggs with the sugar until pale and fluffy, about 5 to 7 minutes. Add the vanilla.

In two additions, add the flour mixture to the egg mixture, scraping down the sides of the bowl between additions. Beat until just combined and uniform.

Stir in the honey mixture.

Pour the cake batter into the prepared baking dish. Bake for 30 to 45 minutes until golden brown and a knife or skewer inserted in the center comes out clean.

While the cake is baking, prepare the milk soak: In a large bowl, stir together all three milks until combined.

Once the cake is done, remove it from the oven and poke holes in it all over with a knife or wooden skewer. Pour one-third of the milk soak all over the cake. It will look like it's drowning. Wait 10 minutes, until the cake has soaked up the milk. Pour another one-third of the milk over the cake. This round will take a little longer to absorb. Once the second round has absorbed, pour the remaining milk soak over the cake. Place the cake in the refrigerator to chill. The cake must be completely cold before topping with the whipped cream.

While the cake is chilling, make the whipped topping (or use Coconut Whipped Cream, recipe follows): In a medium bowl, add the cream, monk fruit sugar, and vanilla. Using a wire whip, or a hand mixer or stand mixer fitted with the whip attachment, beat until medium peaks form.

Once the cake is completely chilled and most of the milk soak has been absorbed, use a rubber spatula to spread the whipped cream over the cake, filling the dish up to the top. Smooth out the topping.

Garnish with toasted coconut flakes and fresh lime zest. Cut into squares, being careful not to smudge the whipped topping, and serve right from the dish.

COCONUT WHIPPED CREAM

Make sure to use a high-quality coconut cream. Refrigerating it overnight will help the texture. Make sure to use a chilled stainless-steel bowl, too, by freezing it for at least 10 minutes before whipping.

- 1 (14-ounce) can coconut cream (I like Nature's Charm Coco Whipping Cream)
- ¼ cup powdered stevia
- ¼ teaspoon vanilla extract

Separate the chilled coconut cream from the liquids in the can and set the liquids aside.

Add the cold, thick coconut cream to a freezer-chilled mixing bowl. Using a hand mixer or wire whip, beat the cream for 1 minute until creamy. Add the powdered stevia and vanilla and continue to beat until smooth and lump-free, about 1 minute more. Cover and return to the refrigerator to chill and set for at least 2 hours but not longer than 2 days.

PLÁTANOS CALADOS

Plantains are used in so many ways in both Latin and Caribbean cuisines that they never go to waste. Because they can be used at all different stages of their ripeness, there is no reason not to prepare something with them. This Colombian favorite translates as Plantains Stewed in Sugar Syrup, and it can be eaten as a dessert or a side dish with fresh farmer's cheese. The plantains must be very ripe for this dish—almost black—so this is often made when you have too many plantains ripening on your counter.

Serves 4

- 1 cup water
- ½ cup coconut sugar or brown monk fruit sugar
- ¼ teaspoon ground nutmeg
- ¼ teaspoon ground allspice
- 1 tablespoon coconut oil
- 1 2-inch piece canela bark or cinnamon stick
- 1 pinch ancho chili powder
- 2 large, very ripe plantains, peeled, halved, and cut into 4 pieces

In a medium pot over medium heat, combine all of the ingredients except the plantains, and bring to a boil. Reduce to a simmer and add the plantains. Cover and cook for 20 minutes or so until the sauce thickens into a syrup and the plantains are cooked through and just tender, not falling apart.

Remove the plantains and let the syrup continue to reduce for 5 minutes more. Remove from the heat.

Set the oven broiler to high.

Place the cooked plantains on a nonstick baking sheet, cut side up. Broil the plantains for 2 to 3 minutes, just until caramelized on the cut side and slightly charred at the edges.

Serve the plantains with the syrup spooned over them. For a real treat, try these with some coconut sorbet or vanilla ice cream!

LEMON CAKE

I love this cake in the springtime, when the need for pumpkin-spice everything finally wanes. Cream cheese frosting is a favorite in my family, usually enjoyed in more decadent applications, but I like this combo of the lighter lemon cake brushed with my homemade Papaya Molasses and topped with just enough frosting. I serve this cake with the frosting gently dolloped all over the top, leaving the sides exposed, and garnished with edible chamomile flowers, though you can use any kind of garnish you like.

Preheat Oven 350°F

Makes 1 (9-inch) cake

Cake:

- Avocado oil spray
- Coconut flour, for preparing the cake pan
- 1 ¾ cups coconut sugar or ¾ cup monk fruit sugar
- Juice of 2 lemons, divided
- Zest of 1 lemon
- ¾ cup avocado oil
- 4 large organic eggs
- 1 cup coconut milk
- 1 teaspoon vanilla extract
- ¾ teaspoon fine sea salt
- 1 ½ cups fine-ground almond flour
- 1 ½ cups coconut flour
- 1 ½ teaspoons baking powder
- 3 tablespoons homemade Papaya Molasses (p. 52) or honey

Frosting:

- 1 cup Cashew Cream Cheese (p. 37) or regular cream cheese
- 1 teaspoon freshly squeezed lemon juice
- 1 teaspoon lemon zest
- ½ cup vegan cashew butter or dairy grass-fed butter
- 1 ½ cups confectioners-style monk fruit sugar or confectioners-style natural stevia sugar

Garnish:

- Loose edible chamomile flowers

Preheat the oven to 350°F. Grease with avocado oil spray and dust with coconut flour a 9-inch round cake pan.

Make the cake: In a stand mixer fitted with the whip attachment, or in a large bowl using a hand mixer with the whip attachment, combine the coconut sugar, juice of one of the lemons and zest, the avocado oil, and eggs. Whip on medium-high speed until pale, and sugar has begun to dissolve, about 4 to 5 minutes. Turn the speed down and carefully add the coconut milk, vanilla, and salt. Turn speed back up and whip for 2 minutes more.

In a separate medium bowl, combine the almond flour, coconut flour, and baking powder.

With the mixer off, add the flour mixture to the egg mixture. Turn the mixer back on and mix until just combined, not more than 30 seconds.

Pour the batter into the prepared baking pan. Bake for 30 minutes or until a knife or skewer inserted in the center comes out clean.

Place the cake in the pan on a rack to begin to cool. Poke holes all over the cake with a knife or skewer.

Stir the Papaya Molasses with the juice from the remaining lemon in a small bowl to combine. Brush the mixture all over the cake in an even layer, allowing it to soak into the cake. Allow the cake to sit for 10 minutes more before carefully removing the cake from the pan and placing on a serving plate right side up. Cool completely before frosting.

Make the frosting: In a stand mixer fitted with the paddle attachment or in a medium bowl with a hand mixer fitted with the beater attachments, beat the Cashew Cream Cheese, lemon juice and zest, cashew butter, and confectioners sweetener until smooth and velvety and the texture of spreadable frosting. Transfer to a piping bag if you want to do a decorative top, or spread over the top of the cake, moving the spatula back and forth in a rustic manner. Garnish as desired.

PUMPKIN "CARROT" CAKE

To be honest, the only reason I ever ate carrot cake was for the frosting, which of course is full of sugar. Carrots are also full of sugar and are folded into a cake with even more sugar! For some reason, people think carrot cake is a healthier cake. Unfortunately, that is not the case, but I've developed a more responsible version. For added crunch, try sprinkling the finished cake with homemade Granola (p. 19).

Preheat Oven 350°F

Makes 1 (9-inch) cake

- Coconut oil spray or avocado oil spray
- ¾ cup almond flour
- ¾ cup coconut flour
- ½ teaspoon baking powder
- ½ teaspoon baking soda
- ½ teaspoon sea salt or pink Himalayan salt
- ¼ teaspoon ground nutmeg
- ¼ teaspoon ground allspice
- ¾ teaspoon ground cinnamon
- 3 large organic eggs
- ¼ cup coconut oil, melted, or grass-fed ghee, melted
- ¼ cup coconut sugar or honey
- ¼ cup coconut cream
- 1 teaspoon vanilla extract
- ¼ teaspoon organic orange extract
- 2 cups peeled, seeded, and grated pumpkin

Frosting:

- 1 cup Cashew Cream Cheese (p. 37)
- 2 tablespoons monk fruit maple syrup
- Pinch of ground cinnamon
- ½ teaspoon lemon zest

Preheat the oven to 350°F. Spray a nonstick 9-inch round cake pan with coconut oil spray.

In a large bowl, add the flours, baking powder, baking soda, salt, and spices. Stir until combined, then set aside.

In a separate bowl, whisk the eggs with the melted oil and coconut sugar until the sugar is dissolved and incorporated into the eggs. Add the coconut cream, vanilla, and orange extract. Stir in the grated pumpkin. Add the wet mix to the dry mix and stir to combine.

Pour the batter into the greased cake pan and bake until a toothpick or knife inserted into the center comes out clean, about 25 to 30 minutes.

Remove the cake from the oven and allow to cool for 15 minutes before popping it out of the pan onto a rack. Allow the cake to cool completely before frosting.

Make the frosting: Combine all the frosting ingredients in a large bowl or the bowl of a stand or handheld electric mixer fitted with the whisk attachment. Whisk by hand or beat on medium speed until smooth and fluffy.

When the cake is completely cooled, dollop the frosting in the center of the cake and, using an offset spatula, spread the frosting out to the edges in a back-and-forth motion, creating decorative rustic waves.

COCOA-AVOCADO MOUSSE

There are few things more decadent than a chocolate mousse, and this doesn't feel any less sinful than the original! Here, the heavy cream is swapped with creamy nutritious avocado and coconut whipping cream and just a touch of agave. This mousse is so rich and creamy you can't tell the difference.

Serves 6

- 1 shot of espresso or 1 teaspoon instant espresso powder
- 1 cup coconut whipping cream, divided
- 1 teaspoon vanilla extract
- 2 tablespoons Dutch cocoa powder
- 8 ounces sugar-free dark chocolate chips (I like Lily's)
- 4 large organic eggs, separated
- 2 medium ripe avocados, peeled and mashed
- 2 tablespoons agave nectar or honey (more if you prefer it sweeter)
- Pinch of sea salt

In the bottom half of a double boiler over medium heat, bring water to a boil. In the top of the double boiler, add the espresso, ½ cup of the coconut whipping cream, vanilla, and cocoa powder. Slowly stir in the chocolate chips until completely melted. Lift the top from the double boiler and set on the counter to cool just slightly, about 3 minutes. The chocolate mixture should still be warm to touch and smooth and pliable. Whisk in the egg yolks until smooth and fully incorporated.

Transfer the warm mixture to a food processor and add the avocado pulp. Pulse and purée until uniform and combined. Spoon into a large bowl and set aside.

In a separate chilled mixing bowl, using a wire whip or a stand or hand mixer fitted with the whip attachment, whip the remaining ½ cup chilled coconut whipping cream with the agave nectar until soft to medium peaks form. Set aside.

In a clean bowl, using a stand mixer, hand mixer, or by hand, whip the egg whites with a pinch of sea salt until stiff peaks form.

Using a rubber spatula, alternate gently folding in the whipped coconut cream, the egg whites, and the chocolate and avocado mixture. Once everything is incorporated and the mixture is uniform, transfer the mousse to individual serving cups or glasses, cover with plastic, and refrigerate to set. Allow to chill for at least 2 hours before serving.

ISLAND TEA-INFUSED NO-MILK FLAN

Many of the Caribbean islands produce some of the best herbal and bush teas. The climate is conducive to growing many varieties. I have always loved infusing teas into my cooking, baking, and curing. Flan is one of my absolute favorite Latin desserts, and the infusion of the Caribbean black passion tea is a nice nuance.

Preheat Oven 350°F

Serves 4

- Coconut oil spray
- ¾ cup coconut sugar or brown monk fruit sugar, divided
- ¼ cup water
- ½ vanilla bean, scraped
- 1 cup unsweetened almond milk
- 1 can (13.5-ounce) coconut milk
- ⅛ teaspoon grated nutmeg
- ⅛ teaspoon fine sea salt
- 1 black passion fruit tea bag
- 4 large organic eggs

Garnish:

- Zest of 1 orange (optional)

Preheat the oven to 350°F. Grease 4 (6-ounce) baking ramekins with coconut oil spray.

Make the caramel base: In a small saucepan, combine ¼ cup of the coconut sugar with ¼ cup of water. Heat over medium-high heat, stirring, until the sugar dissolves and turns a golden brown caramel color. While the caramel is still hot, divide and pour it into the prepared ramekins.

Make the custard: In another small saucepan over medium heat, combine the vanilla bean, almond milk, and coconut milk along with the nutmeg, salt, and the tea bag. Bring the mixture to a boil and immediately reduce to a simmer. Cook for 2 minutes. Remove from heat and allow to steep for 3 minutes.

In a medium bowl by hand, or with a handheld electric mixer, beat the eggs and remaining ½ cup coconut sugar together until pale and fluffy and doubled in size, about 3 to 5 minutes. Remove the tea bag from the hot milk mixture and slowly whisk into the eggs, tempering a little bit at a time to avoid cooking the eggs. Pour the mixture through a fine-mesh strainer into a pitcher.

Divide and pour the custard base into the ramekins. Place the ramekins into a baking pan. Carefully pour boiling water into the baking pan until the water reaches halfway up the base of the ramekins. Be careful not to get water in the custard.

Bake for 1 hour or until just set. The flan should feel firm to the touch with your finger, but not solid, and lightly colored. Remove the baking pan from the oven and allow the custards to cool in the tray for at least 30 minutes. Remove the ramekins, cover with plastic, and refrigerate for at least 4 hours or overnight before serving.

Using a small offset spatula or a butter knife, gently loosen the edges of the flan before turning out upside down onto the serving plates. The caramel sauce should ooze out right when you flip the flans onto the plates.

Garnish with a dusting of orange zest if desired.

HOMEMADE NUT BUTTER COOKIES

You can make these cookies using any one of the Homemade Nut Butter recipes from the Mornings chapter, but you can also make them with store-bought almond or peanut butter. Just make sure to use a good raw product, avoiding processed butters with sugar and other additives. Having these cookies on hand for late-night cravings is great, or for an afternoon treat with a cup of tea.

Preheat Oven 350°F

Makes 24 cookies

- 1 ½ cups Homemade Nut Butter (p. 51) or store-bought nut butter of choice
- ½ cup coconut sugar or brown Swerve
- 2 large organic eggs
- ¼ cup coconut flour

Preheat the oven to 350°F. Grease a nonstick baking sheet with coconut oil spray.

Using an electric mixer with paddle attachment, or in a mixing bowl with a wooden spoon, combine all ingredients and stir until thickened and uniform.

Divide the dough into 24 portions, rolling each into a ball.

Spread the balls out, at least 2 inches apart, on the prepared baking sheet. Flatten each ball halfway into a disk using your thumb, then flatten the rest of the way using a fork in a cross hatch pattern until the cookies are about ¼ inch thick.

Bake the cookies for 15 minutes. Remove from oven and cool for 5 minutes before removing from the baking sheet and transferring to a cooling rack.

Enjoy while they are still warm or cool completely before storing for up to one week in an airtight container.

COCKTAILS (BEBIDAS)

When it comes to drinking booze, there is no real "healthy" version, but creating healthier versions of cocktails at least makes for some enjoyment in moderation. More important to me than trying to drink less at one sitting is to drink less often. Don't drink every time you go out to dinner, but when you do, don't count the carbs and calories. Pick a night, pick one of these healthier recipes, and make a few drinks and enjoy yourself. Trust me, you will do more harm to your nutritional plan drinking one glass of wine or straight spirits every night than if you have a free drinking night once a week.

- Yucatán Michelada
- Spicy Papaya Margarita
- The Smoking Dragon Fruit
- Strawberry-Ginger Mojito
- Coco-Lime Margarita
- Dark and Not So Stormy
- Sangria
- Coconut Sugar Simple Syrup
- Coconut-Infused Bourbon
- Coc-old Fashioned
- Canchánchara with Prickly Pear
- Spicy Infused Reposado Tequila

YUCÁTAN MICHELADA

There are numerous variations of this classic Mexican drink, all of which are certain to quench your thirst on a hot day. A combination of ice-cold beer, different sauces, spices, and lime, Micheladas hit the spot. An ice-cold chilled beer glass works best.

Serves 1

- Pink Himalayan salt
- ½ teaspoon Valentina hot sauce
- ¼ teaspoon Tabasco (2 dashes)
- 1 teaspoon Maggi seasoning
- ½ teaspoon Worcestershire sauce
- 1 tablespoon freshly squeezed lime juice
- 2 fresh ripe cherry or grape tomatoes
- Crushed ice
- Light Mexican beer

Garnishes:

- Fresh lime wedges
- Fresh oregano sprig

Using a lime wedge, moisten the rim of a chilled tall beer mug. Pour the pink salt onto a plate and dip the rim of the beer mug into the salt to rim it. Add the Valentina, Tabasco, Maggi, Worcestershire, lime juice, and tomatoes, and muddle right in the glass for 30 seconds to smash up the tomatoes and combine the flavors. Add enough crushed ice to fill the glass. Pour over the light Mexican beer and garnish with limes and oregano sprig. Serve the rest of the beer on the side.

SPICY PAPAYA MARGARITA

You would be hard-pressed to go to a bar these days and not find a spicy margarita on the menu—and for good reason. Spicy variations of the classic party cocktail are here to stay. I particularly like this combination with the papaya, enhancing the nuances of the spice, almost reminiscent of street fruits sprinkled with lime and chile de árbol powder.

Serves 1

Chile-Lime Salt:
- 2 dried pasilla negro chile peppers
- 2 tablespoons pink Himalayan salt
- Zest of 2 limes
- Zest of 1 orange

Margarita:
- 1 ounce spicy Infused reposado tequila (p. 180)
- ½ ounce additional (not infused) reposado tequila
- ½ ounce freshly squeezed lime juice
- ¼ ounce orange liqueur such as Cointreau or Curacao
- ½ cup puréed fresh papaya
- 1 cup ice

Garnishes:
- Lime wedges

Make the Chile-Lime Salt: In a dry cast-iron skillet, toast the pasilla chiles over medium heat for 2 to 3 minutes until fragrant and beginning to smoke. Remove from heat and cool completely. Open the chiles and remove the seeds. Place the peppers into a spice grinder or high-powered blender and pulse into a powder. Combine the ground chiles, salt, and citrus zests. Store in an airtight container for up to two weeks.

For the Margarita: Moisten the rim of a rocks or margarita glass with a lime wedge. Pour the Chile-Lime Salt onto a plate and dredge the rim in the salt. In a cocktail shaker, combine the infused tequila, additional tequila, lime juice, orange liqueur, papaya purée, and ice. Shake well for 20 seconds. Pour all of the contents into the glass as is, and top with additional ice as needed. Garnish with a floating lime wedge.

THE SMOKING DRAGON FRUIT

Serves 1
- 2 ounces Scotch whisky
- 1 ½ ounces fresh dragon fruit juice or prickly pear juice
- ¾ ounce honey syrup (equal parts purified water and honey)
- 1 ounce freshly squeezed lemon juice
- 1 cup ice

Garnish:
- Lemon wheel

Those who know me best know that I am a scotch enthusiast. I love the combination of the smoky scotch against the earthy subtly sweet dragon fruit, not to mention how pretty it is. I rarely like to mix a good scotch with anything, but for this drink, it's worth it.

If you have a juicer, great! If not, purée the fruit and push through a fine-mesh strainer to extract the juice.

Combine all ingredients in a cocktail shaker. Shake vigorously for 20 seconds. Fine-strain the drink into a coupe glass and garnish with a floating lemon wheel.

STRAWBERRY-GINGER MOJITO

The standard variation for a ginger mojito would be to use a good ginger beer in place of the usual club soda topper. But here we use fresh ginger in order to omit the high sugar content.

Serves 1

- 2 strawberries, stemmed and halved
- ½ teaspoon coconut sugar or brown Swerve
- 1 (⅛-inch) slice fresh ginger root
- 4 fresh mint leaves
- 1 ½ ounces white light rum
- 1 ounce freshly squeezed lime juice
- Crushed ice
- Club soda

Garnish:

- Fresh mint sprigs

In a tall Collins glass or tumbler, add the strawberries, coconut sugar, ginger root, mint, and rum. Muddle well for 20 to 30 seconds. Add the lime juice and fill the glass with crushed ice. Finish with club soda and garnish with fresh mint sprigs.

COCO-LIME MARGARITA

This is by far my favorite variation on a margarita, especially in the heat of the summer—preferably on a beach somewhere. This satisfies that coco flavor profile I used to indulge in piña coladas, in a much lighter format. Plus, too much rum is never a good thing. This recipe includes a coconut sugar version of traditional simple syrup. I prefer to hand-stir all my simple syrups. Introducing heat changes the profile, and the ration starts to break down as water evaporates.

Serves 1

- 2 ounces coconut cream
- 2 ounces blanco tequila
- 1 ounce freshly squeezed lime juice
- ½ ounce freshly squeezed orange juice
- ¼ ounce Coconut Sugar Simple Syrup (p. 161)
- Ice for shaker, plus 1 large ice cube

Garnishes:

- Fresh lime zest
- Star fruit

Combine the coconut cream, tequila, lime juice, orange juice, and Coconut Sugar Simple Syrup in a cocktail shaker with ice. Shake vigorously for 10 to 25 seconds. Strain and pour over one large cube of ice.

Garnish by zesting fresh lime zest all over the edges of the drink and half of the rim. Wedge a slice of star fruit on the rim.

DARK AND NOT SO STORMY

The unofficial drink of Bermuda, rightfully named because of its eerie storm-like appearance, is one of my favorites for sure. The balance of the sharp spicy bite of ginger beer against the molasses flavor of Gosling's Black Seal rum is a perfect maritime marriage. But, as much as I love ginger beer, the average glass has almost 40 grams of sugar! A variation of bubbly water and fresh ginger does the trick in this lighter riff.

Serves 1

- 1 slice fresh ginger root, about ¼ inch thick
- ¼ ounce Coconut Sugar Simple Syrup (p. 161)
- 2 ounces Gosling's Black Seal rum
- ½ ounce freshly squeezed lime juice
- 4 or 5 ounces club soda or Pellegrino sparkling mineral water

Garnishes:
- Lime wedge
- Fresh mint sprig

In a tall Collins glass or pint glass, muddle the fresh ginger slice with the Coconut Sugar Simple Syrup.

Add the rum and lime juice, and fill the glass with ice. Top off with club soda or Pellegrino, and garnish with a lime wedge and mint sprig.

SANGRIA

Although Sangria originates from Spain, Latin America has embraced this refreshing beverage, even creating its own version called Clerico, most often made with white wine or rose instead of Spain's traditional red wine. Traditionally, whether making a red or white Sangria or Clerico, fruit juice or lemonade is added as a sweetener. I have opted out of using juice in the below version, and instead added some spicy liqueur, but if you aren't a fan feel free to sub back in a fresh juice such as fresh squeezed orange juice or pomegranate juice. I recommend making the mix and letting it sit overnight before serving, giving the fruits time to soak up some wine!

Serves 4

- 4 cups dry red wine
- ½ cup Ancho Reyes verde, chile poblano liqueur
- ½ cup fresh lime juice
- 1 cup cubed papaya (1-inch pieces)
- 1 cup cubed cantaloupe (1-inch pieces)
- 1 orange, quartered and sliced thin
- 3 or 4 sprigs fresh mint
- Lots of ice

Combine all ingredients except ice in a pitcher and stir to combine. Allow to chill for at least 45 minutes before serving. Pour into wineglasses over ice.

COCONUT SUGAR SIMPLE SYRUP

This is an important staple in my house. So many cocktails call for simple syrup, and this is a nice, subtle, less-processed version. Coconut sugar is not only lower in carbs and less sweet to taste, it also adds a nice layer of flavor to most cocktails, especially tropical based classics.

- 1 cup coconut sugar
- 1 cup purified water

In a large measuring cup or jar, combine the coconut sugar and purified water. Stir until the sugar is dissolved. You can let it sit for about 20 to 30 minutes and stir again to break down any bits of sugar left. Strain and store in an airtight container, refrigerated.

COCONUT-INFUSED BOURBON

In the cocktail world this process is referred to as fat washing. Fats and oils are wonderful conduits for flavor and this process can be done with a wide variety of ingredients. The key being to first infuse the oil or fat with the desired flavor ingredient before adding to the spirit. Try playing around with other aromatics into the coconut oil for added layers of flavor.

Makes 1 liter
- 2 ounces unsweetened coconut flakes
- 1 ounce virgin coconut oil
- 1 liter bourbon of choice

In a small sauté pan over medium heat, toast the coconut, stirring often, until golden, about 5 minutes. Remove from heat and immediately add the coconut oil, swirling to stop the coconut flakes from cooking. Allow to cool just slightly.

In a plastic Cambro or jug, combine the bourbon and the coconut mixture, and whisk well. Allow to sit at room temperature for 2 hours.

Transfer the mixture to the freezer, and freeze for 24 hours. This will solidify the fatty coconut oil, allowing for easy straining.

Pull the mixture out of the freezer and strain through a fine-mesh strainer lined with cheesecloth. Pour the coconut bourbon back into its original bottle and refrigerate until ready to use, for up to 6 months if refrigerated.

COC-OLD FASHIONED

Fat washing spirits is a fun way to infuse flavors into your liquor without adulterating the clarity and texture. This a great subtle riff on a classic, timeless cocktail.

Serves 1

- 1 teaspoon coconut sugar
- 2 dashes angostura bitters
- 1 dash chocolate bitters
- 2 ounces Coconut-Infused Bourbon (p. 178)

Garnishes:

- Key lime twist
- Orange twist

Muddle the coconut sugar and the two bitters in an old-fashioned glass for about 10 to 15 seconds. Add the Coconut-Infused Bourbon and one large ice cube. Stir until well chilled. Garnish with key lime and orange twists.

CANCHÁNCHARA with PRICKLY PEAR

This simple refreshing drink, originating actually from Trinidad, is said to be Cuba's oldest known cocktail adaptation. I have brightened it up here with the addition of prickly pear, a beloved fruit of the desert lands, also known as cactus flower.

Serves 1

- 2 ounces white rum
- 1 ounce freshly squeezed lime juice
- ½ ounce fresh prickly pear, peeled and chopped
- ½ ounce honey syrup (equal parts honey and purified water)
- Club soda

Garnish:

- Lime wheel

Add rum, lime juice, prickly pear, and honey syrup to a cocktail shaker with ice and shake well until chilled, about 15 seconds.

Strain into a stemless wineglass filled with fresh ice.

Top with club soda, and garnish with a floating lime wheel.

SPICY INFUSED REPOSADO TEQUILA

I absolutely love a spicy cocktail, so naturally I had to include one in my book. Infusing the tequila ahead of time is nice convenient way to add heat to a drink without having to mess around with chiles in the moment. There are so many chiles in the world, the flavor combinations are endless! Try adding a smokey dried chile such as Pasilla Negro or Ancho.

Makes 750 milliliters

- 1 (750-milliliter) bottle reposado tequila (I like Hiatus)
- 3 Scotch bonnet or habanero peppers, halved

Combine the reposado tequila and peppers in a quart container or pitcher. Cover and infuse for 24 hours at room temperature. Strain through a fine-mesh strainer back into the tequila bottle, and keep for up to 1 month at room temperature.

ACKNOWLEDGMENTS

To thank all of the wonderful people who have given me their time and energy over the years is a very paramount task.

First and foremost, I'd like to thank my mom and dad. I am profoundly grateful for their support in my career choice, and for sticking with me through this ride.

To my Mimi, I miss you eternally and think of you every day that I step foot in a kitchen. I know you are watching down on me.

Thank you to my dearest husband, Alexander, for supporting me and for always eating my food and giving me your valuable brutally honest feedback.

To Gordon Ramsay, thank you for giving me the opportunity to connect with the world (twice), and for inspiring me to fight to the finish no matter what the task and to always strive for excellence. Thank you to all of my chef mentors and restaurateurs throughout my career who were gracious enough to share their knowledge with me and help me rise up through the ranks: Joseph Manzare and Robert Roaquin from Globe back in the day, Larry Nicola and "Smiley" from Nic's, Todd Mark Miller from STK, Mads Refslund from Acme, Ken Halberg and Spencer Slaine from Harding's, Michael Cory from OTG, and all of the amazing chef partners I got to open thirty-six unique concepts with: Mario Carbone, Jose Garces, Dale Talde, Amanda Freitag, Josh Capon, Marc Forgione. Thank you for having me train in your kitchens!

To Keith Beitler, thank you for motivating me to work hard, and for believing in me. You inspire me to do the right thing always, even when nobody is watching.

Christina Wilson, you are a force to be reckoned with. You are an inspiration!

To Andy and Julia, thank you for giving me my first job on a farm. This is where it all started.

To my beautiful girls, London and Charlotte, for your patience while Mommy is always working!

To all of my fans and restaurant enthusiasts, without your continued interest in my journey, I would not have been able to share this book with the world!

And lastly, thank you to all moms, grandmothers, and great-grandmothers who live in the beloved countries and islands of my heritage: for passing down from generation to generation the recipes that inspired me to write this book. I hope you don't mind my new healthier takes.

Ariel

ABOUT THE AUTHOR

Chef Ariel Fox has joined the ranks of the fierce female forces of Manhattan's illustrious dining scene. Her culinary philosophy stems from her teenage years in Northern California, where she worked for the small, family-run Mariquita Farm in Watsonville. It was there that Chef Ariel was first introduced to sustainable food movement pioneer Alice Waters. Waters sparked Chef Ariel's profound appreciation for organic agriculture and seasonal food. Undeniably, Ariel's Afro-Latino and Caribbean heritage has been her other leading inspiration in her cuisine from the beginning. Since then, Chef Ariel's career has taken her from coast to coast, and today, as Vice President of Culinary for Landry's, and coauthor of Freckle-Faced Foodie: Journey of a Young Chef, Chef Ariel's passion for fresh, seasonal ingredients remains the cornerstone of her celebrated cuisine. A graduate of the California School of Culinary Arts, Chef Ariel's first gig was as a line cook at the Venice Beach celebrity haunt Globe. In 2006 she was named chef de cuisine at the acclaimed restaurant Nic's in Beverly Hills.

Chef Ariel was part of the opening team of STK in West Hollywood in 2007 and soon thereafter was appointed as the executive sous chef for STK's parent hospitality company, The ONE Group. In her new role, Chef Ariel launched multiple ONE Group restaurants, streamlining the culinary programs for STK outposts in Las Vegas, Miami, and midtown Manhattan.

In 2008, Chef Ariel was selected to compete on Hell's Kitchen, the smash FOX television series hosted by celebrity chef Gordon Ramsay, and became a top-three finalist. She was invited back to compete on Hell's Kitchen eleven years later and walked out with the win. Chef Ariel has also appeared on VH1, Good Day LA and Good Day New York, and holds a repeat guest chef role on the hit Food Network series Beat Bobby Flay. Chef Ariel now resides in New Jersey with her husband Alexander, daughter Charlotte Grace, and stepdaughter London. She continues to strive for excellence as she rapidly cements her place as a powerful voice in the next generation of culinary professionals.

Kingston Imperial

Marvis Johnson – Publisher
Joshua Wirth – Designer
Rachel Jensen – Publicist, Finn Partners
Sharon Farnell – Publicist, Finn Partners
Roby Marcondes – Marketing Manager

Contact:
Email: Info@kingstonimperial.com
www.kingstonimperial.com

For information address Kingston Imperial, LLC Rights Department, info@kingstonimperial.com

Published by Kingston Imperial, LLC
www.kingstonimperial.com

Cataloging in Publication data is on file with the Library of Congress.

Spice Kitchen: Healthy Latin And Caribbean Cuisine by Ariel Fox. Foreword by Gordon Ramsay.

Photographs by Teddy Wolff

Styling by Jamie Kimm

Book Design by Joshua Wirth of PiXiLL Designs, LLC

Printed in China

First Edition

Hardcover ISBN: 9781954220249
Ebook ISBN: 9781954220256